Women and IPM

Crop protection practices and strategies

Elske van de Fliert and Jet Proost (eds.)

Women and IPM

Crop protection practices and strategies

Royal Tropical Institute

Intermediate Technology Publications

Practical Action Publishing Ltd
25 Albert Street, Rugby, CV21 2SD, Warwickshire, UK
www.practicalactionpublishing.org

© Intermediate Technology Publications 1999

First published 1999\Digitised 2013

ISBN 10: 1 85339 482 3
ISBN 13: 9781853394829
ISBN Library Ebook: 9781780445670
Book DOI: http://dx.doi.org/10.3362/9781780445670

All rights reserved. No part of this publication may be reprinted or reproduced or utilized in any form or by any electronic, mechanical, or other means, now known or hereafter invented, including photocopying and recording, or in any information storage or retrieval system, without the written permission of the publishers.

A catalogue record for this book is available from the British Library.

The authors, contributors and/or editors have asserted their rights under the Copyright Designs and Patents Act 1988 to be identified as authors of their respective contributions.

Since 1974, Practical Action Publishing has published and disseminated books and information in support of international development work throughout the world. Practical Action Publishing is a trading name of Practical Action Publishing Ltd (Company Reg. No. 1159018), the wholly owned publishing company of Practical Action. Practical Action Publishing trades only in support of its parent charity objectives and any profits are covenanted back to Practical Action (Charity Reg. No. 247257, Group VAT Registration No. 880 9924 76).

Table of contents

Acknowledgements	7
Foreword Jan C. Zadoks	9
Introduction	11
1 The struggle against pesticides Sarojeni V. Rengam	15
2 Russian women's roles in crop protection in the new agricultural economy Sarah J. Tisch and Natalia Poznanskaya	23
3 Women in plant protection in Zanzibar Alida A. Laurense and Fadhila H. Ali	31
4 Establishing gender sensitive IPM: a cowpea programme in Ghana Brenda J. Vander Mey	39
5 Women's roles in crop protection decision making: the case of Atenas County, Costa Rica Lisa Bradshaw	51
6 Improving women's participation in pest management training: a pilot study in Honduras Catrin J. Meir	59
7 Women in IPM training and implementation in Indonesia Elske van de Fliert	71
8 Women in Vietnam's National IPM Programme Nguyen Nhat Tuyen	79
9 Gender aspects of IPM for citrus in eastern Bhutan Frank H.J. van Schoubroeck, Cheki Wangmo and B.B. Acharya	89
Epilogue Janice Jiggins	101
About the authors	105

Acknowledgements

This book originated in the preparations for the 13th International Plant Protection Congress (The Hague, 1995), when Professor Zadoks, the congress organizer, requested the editors to organize and convene a symposium on Gender Issues and Crop Protection. This was the first time this generally technical congress had included a symposium on gender issues. However, although gender is a hot topic in most development projects, finding speakers with substantial experience who could say something specific about the relation between gender and crop protection was somewhat problematical. The field is new enough that little literature was available. Crop protection specialists usually have a technical background, and not uncommonly find it hard to deal with social issues. Gender specialists generally have a social science background, often not being involved in the technical side of programmes. Nevertheless, eight people were found to present experiences from a variety of countries spread over four different continents; two additional posters were also presented. The symposium, including a networking session at the end of the day, provided a unique opportunity for those interested in gender and crop protection to share experiences, develop new ideas together and thus push this relatively new and immature field several steps ahead.

To follow up on the momentum gained at the congress, it was decided to publish the symposium papers for distribution among the network and beyond. Rather than simply collecting the papers as proceedings, an attempt has been made to provide a multidimensional exposition on the topic of gender and crop protection. Oral and poster presentations from the symposium have been revised to fit the structure of the book, and an analytic epilogue has been added. We would like to thank Kitty Hovenkamp for reviewing previous versions of the papers, and are happy to have been able to work with KIT Press to facilitate wider distribution of these first experiences in gender and crop protection. We especially appreciate the critical comments from the Press and others within the Royal Tropical Institute. Additionally, we are grateful to the authors for their willingness to revise their papers one or more times to produce the present chapters, and to Janice Jiggins, Professor of Human Ecology at the University of Agricultural Sciences, Uppsala, Sweden, who has provided the broader view presented in the Epilogue.

Elske van de Fliert
Jet Proost

Foreword: the gender issue in crop protection

'Please meet the farmer and her husband' is a worn quip containing a great deal of truth. Millions of farmers are women, and given the many absentee male farmers who find they can earn more in non-rural occupations, their numbers are increasing.

Similarly, decision making on the farm is becoming less a male-only affair for several reasons, of which male absenteeism is only one. Women usually participate actively in crop protection, doing manual weeding and routing out insects. They nearly always manage the home garden that provides the family's vegetables; sometimes they manage the market garden as well. Often women take care of seed storage. All over the world, many women hold the purse strings and thus have a say in purchases related to crop protection.

In most developing countries, gender separation is more apparent than elsewhere. Division of labour between genders may reach a level such that when a scientist or surveyor poses a question to a woman, the answer comes back from a man. The resulting distortion of information can be considerable. For example, women farmers' knowledge of crop protection issues and women's influence on crop protection decisions may thus have remained hidden.

Men's and women's training and frame of reference may differ considerably. In addition, farm women and women farmers in developing countries are very busy people. They are responsible for home and garden, for rearing the children and feeding the family, for water and fuel, and they work on the land. As a result, the time available to women for crop protection training is strictly limited in duration and time-of-day, and while not necessarily inferior the knowledge base of women farmers entering a training course may differ from that of male farmers.

The 13th International Plant Protection Congress, The Hague, 1995, officially acknowledged these facts, which so far have been ignored by formal crop protection science. As a part of the Congress, a special session on 'Gender issues in crop protection' was organized, of which this book is the scientific precipitate. As a scientific endeavour this book represents an exploratory phase, primarily presenting casuistics, with a touch of theory kindly added by Professor Janice Jiggins.

On behalf of the IPPC, I thank the authors for their worthwhile contributions and the editors, Elske van de Fliert and Jet Proost, for their painstaking and time-consuming efforts.

J.C. Zadoks
Organizer
13th International Plant Protection Congress

Introduction

In the developing world, day to day crop management is often women's work: women are thus the ones who are the most likely to see pests and their effects. Yet in the countries covered in this book as elsewhere, women are generally assigned the hardest, most back-breaking and labour intensive tasks, which often also pay the least. Women's important role in agriculture often remains invisible, and their knowledge is often ignored instead of being put to use in agricultural decision making. In addition to empowerment and equity, this is an important reason for increasing attention to social aspects, including gender and gender roles in communities. Involving women can provide significant support to IPM crop protection programmes; as the following chapters demonstrate, taking these factors into account is not 'just another trend', but a necessity.

Although this book originated in a conference on plant protection, the majority of chapters relate to integrated pest management (IPM). IPM was initially seen as a strategy to attack a single pest, combining all available control techniques in a compatible manner and using pesticides as a last resort. Over the past decade, IPM has developed into a more holistic approach, in which the pest complex in a crop is considered as a whole, with ecological processes that already exist in the agroecosystem being encouraged to do most of the work (van de Fliert, 1998). Pesticide use is avoided to keep from disturbing the ecological balance. Considering the developments in many IPM programmes over the last decade, which have emphasized empowering farmers as pest management decision makers rather than consumers of technologies developed by far-away research institutes (van de Fliert, 1998), it is clear that information and training are necessary. Good IPM farmers are expected to be ecosystem managers and independent experts in their own fields. This approach requires specific knowledge, observation and decision making skills, as well as problem-solving capacity on the part of farmers. Regular observation and analysis, plus condition-specific experimentation are the primary tools to be used in obtaining the information needed to take decisions. Intensive training is needed for farmers to acquire such IPM knowledge and skills. What is surprising, for a holistic approach, is that often insufficient attention has been given to involving women in this training. The cases recounted here demonstrate not only that such attention is needed, but also that it supports field-level implementation of IPM.

The following chapters offer several practical lessons on women's roles in crop protection and ways to increase their access to IPM information and training. These go beyond the question of making training programmes more accessible to women; they raise the related issues of who has the power to design a course or select trainers and participants, and who holds the expert knowledge or the jobs within the official hierarchy. The cases also show the interrelationships among social structures, power relations, and processes such as the privatization of farm services that may accompany changes in farm cooperatives. They provide not only clear analyses of situations, but also strategies for change.

The first two chapters focus on the general involvement of women in crop protection practices based on use of pesticides. As Rengam demonstrates in Chapter 1, women are exposed to pesticide hazards while lacking sufficient access to information and services. Conclusions and recommendations from a survey carried out in seven Asian countries provide insight into the irresponsible risks being taken and the urgency of action and change. It is crucial to recognize and value women's invaluable labour, skills and knowledge regarding crop protection. In Chapter 2, Tisch and Poznanskaya picture the situation in Russia. Women, who played dominant roles in both plant protection practice and research in the former Soviet agroindustrial system, are being replaced by men in positions other than that of labourer. Reduced budgets and scarcity of inputs followed the 1989 structural changes in what were previously collective farms; agricultural yields have decreased, and diseases and weeds are spreading. The continuing dependence on crop protection chemicals is striking. If crop yields are to be maintained and increased, changes in strategies for field crop protection will be needed. Implicit in this chapter is the intriguing possibility of combining the essential recognition of women's roles with the initiation of an IPM approach.

Chapter 3 shows a related situation in Zanzibar. Laurense and Ali point out that as in many other African countries, women predominate in the work of food crop production, and it is typically their responsibility to make sure the family has enough to eat for the day. Yet no women serve as extension officers at village level, and almost none at other levels or as researchers or policymakers. This is very unfortunate since female extension workers, researchers and decision makers can be key players in improving the agricultural skills of African farmers, and particularly women farmers – not only in direct training but also in policymaking. To change the situation, job opportunities and promotions for women will also be needed. Laurense and Ali point out how more women extension officers can be trained and employed in rural communities. Laurense and Ali see IPM as an approach *par excellence* for women. Cultural control methods like planting, weeding and close monitoring of crops are women's activities, as are selection of seeds and planting material. However, to be effective, training directed towards women will be needed, requiring institutional changes in the national research, development and extension systems.

Chapter 4 begins with a strong statement from Vander Mey about the importance of women's realities and roles in agriculture, and a discussion of the promise of IPM. The chapter further describes the planning and early implementation of the gender sensitive Clemson/Ghana IPM on Cowpea Project in Ghana, where these ideas are being put into practice. Interviews with farmers and pilot IPM implementors were used to understand women's special needs within the gendered family farming system. This project involves US and Ghanaian research teams; both include women, as do those involved in the training of trainers.

Bradshaw, in Chapter 5, presents a case study from Costa Rica, where farm size is shrinking and as elsewhere structural adjustment programmes have had a major impact. As men go to better paying jobs outside the village, women have become increasingly involved in agriculture. In addition, changing social policy is creating access to agricultural credits and property rights for women. Yet, in spite of their work with crops and livestock, many women do not immediately see themselves as 'farmers'. They seem interested, and crop protection is a topic of conversation among women, but access to crop protection information and training is low. Factors that prevent women from gaining access to pest management information are explored and opportunities for increasing women's knowledge and participation in crop protection training are recommended.

The question of women's access to IPM extension information and training, as well as ways to enhance their active participation, is further addressed in Chapter 6. Here Meir emphasizes that organizing training in women's home communities and at times that suit them is vital, just as is addressing women's specific needs and opportunities for implementation. This study in Honduras follows the progress of a natural control training course for women, in a context where women are offered little opportunity to participate in pest management training due to a strong dichotomy in the roles of women and men. Comparisons, including the impact six months later, between the two communities involved make it possible to draw quite specific lessons. As this chapter makes clear, women are important innovators and are quite interested in reducing the use of pesticides when they have an opportunity to learn how to do this.

In Chapter 7, van de Fliert describes how cultural habits led to the unequal representation of women in IPM Farmer Field Schools, especially during the programme's first training cycles, even though in most places these habits were not necessarily cultural barriers. Special efforts within the National Programme to train IPM trainers to facilitate a training preparation process, including the use of a village-level gender analysis, resulted in a considerable increase in women participants in IPM Farmer Field Schools, although the national average target of 25% has still not been achieved. More intensive training for and application of the preparation process is needed to further enhance women's access to and role in the Field Schools.

Chapter 8, by Nguyen Nhat Tuyen, describes the National IPM Programme in Vietnam, which in principle provides access to training for women. However, their participation in crop protection courses was found to be not at all equal to that of men, even though the majority work in the agricultural sector and a significant number of farm households are headed by women. A study by the Centre for Family and Women's Studies showed a number of factors that hamper women's attendance, as well as variations by geographic region, based on customs and gender relations. The perception and understanding of women's roles and responsibilities by leaders and trainers at all levels appears to be a key issue. Since the degree and quality of women's participation in IPM programmes depends greatly on the gender sensitivity of decision makers, the recommendation is to build this in from the start, in planning at national and local levels as well as in the selection of participants and training methods, and through collaboration with women's organizations. In most areas of Indonesia women play an important role in crop production, but - even though they play an important role in family decision making, and even though many IPM practices relate to farm responsibilities held by women - initially they were seldom selected to participate in National IPM Programme training.

Finally, Chapter 9 portrays the evolution of gendered aspects of a citrus IPM programme in Bhutan. Van Schoubroeck, Wangmo and Acharya describe an IPM programme that began without specific attention to gender and the related dynamics of village organization, but came to recognize that building in these elements was essential to programme success. Gender segregated information then came to be used as a tool for more effective programme planning and implementation: women helped to embed IPM in village life. This study shows clearly that fighting the Chinese citrus fly technically was one factor, but that sociocultural aspects can be even more important. Here a culturally appropriate way was found to give trained women a new status by appointing them as 'mandarin leaders'. This allowed them to make use of their training in the community. Further, mixed staff patterns were found useful, but here the sex of the extension staff appeared to be irrelevant compared to the value of speaking the local language and respecting local customs.

Although attention to gender issues would, strictly speaking, imply attention not only to women's roles but also to those of men (de Bruyn, 1995), the papers in this book refer primarily to women. This is a reaction to the common occurrence of technical activities (among which crop protection is generally classified) in which men are the main actors: deliberate action is needed to bring women into the picture. As Jiggins points out very clearly in the Epilogue, gender analysis is not simply *en vogue*; it is crucial for those working on improving the potential of agriculture, and crop protection strategies in particular. Yet most papers describe activities at a new frontier, in which deliberate attention to women is still needed to induce basic changes in perception. A shift towards the application of more balanced, gendered strategies can already be observed in the more mature programmes, such as those in Indonesia, Vietnam, Ghana and Bhutan.

These chapters can thus be seen as pioneering efforts, perhaps not always entirely fulfilling scientific requirements but nevertheless reflecting the situation in a number of countries. The book is intended to share gender and crop protection experiences on a wider scale, and to illustrate the importance of involving women in decision making as well as implementation and dissemination. In many cases it also demonstrates the continuing need for integrated pest management as a crop protection strategy with the potential to enhance the sustainability of small farm enterprises, hence improving the livelihoods of rural women. Our hope, however, is not only to spread the knowledge and insights now being gathered in specific parts of the world, but also to inspire others. We hope this material will trigger more substantial, scientific research on the gender related aspects of the development of pest management strategies, and of IPM in particular.

Bibliography

Bruyn, de M. (ed.), *Advancing women's status: women and men together?* Critical reviews and a selected annotated bibliography. Amsterdam, Royal Tropical Institute, 1995.

Fliert, van de E., Integrated pest management: springboard to sustainable agriculture. In: G.S. Dhaliwal and E.A. Heinrichs (eds.), *Critical issues in insect pest management*. New Delhi, Commonwealth Publishers, 1998, pp. 250–266.

Sarojeni V. Rengam[1]

1 The struggle against pesticides

> Bilkis, three months pregnant, picks cotton in the fields while her husband sprays pesticides. She is barefoot and uses no protective clothing. After working in the fields she feeds the animals, changes her clothes and hangs up those she has worn to use during the following day's work in the fields. The next day she continues. When she is giddy she takes a fifteen-minute break and then goes on working. She explains: 'When we enter the field for the first picking, it is extremely suffocating. In fact, the whole village stinks with the smell of pesticides'.

> Joy, from the Philippines, has a terrible itch that affects her hips and legs; it has persisted for more than a month. She has tried all sorts of creams the shop owner recommended but to no avail. She cannot afford to take time off from work on the farm to go to the nearest clinic – it is a two-hour bus ride from where she lives. She has just had to learn to live with it, but is sure it is caused by the pesticides she applies to her rice plot each week.

In rural Asia, the use of pesticides has permeated even the remotest village. The availability of highly toxic pesticides, combined with a lack of information (including knowledge of their hazards) and aggressive marketing by the industry, plus poverty, illiteracy, and the lack of health facilities in rural areas, ensure that pesticides are a major cause of poisoning in farming communities.

It is thus not surprising that in the South alone an estimated 25 million workers and farmers have been poisoned by pesticides (Jeyaratnam, 1990) in past years. Farmers and agricultural workers are exposed directly when they mix and spray pesticides. Contamination of the soil, air and water insidiously exposes communities and consumers as well. The chronic effects are particularly alarming in the light of new studies linking certain pesticides to cancer and decreases in fertility (Hileman, 1994 and Soto, 1993) including a drop in sperm quality and quantity (Danish EPA, 1995). Other studies have shown that women with relatively high levels of estrogen imitators in their blood are far more likely to develop breast cancer than women with relatively low levels (Soto, 1993). General immune system suppression has also been noted (Repetto and Baliga, 1996).

The culture of silence

For the millions of women farming the land, exposure to pesticide hazards is nothing new. Women in Asia make up 50–60% of the agricultural workforce; in some countries the figure is as high as 80–90%. In agriculture, women are involved in all stages of seed and land preparation, planting, weeding, harvesting, storage, seed conservation and exchange, processing and finally marketing and cooking. They generally carry out the hardest, most back-breaking and labour intensive tasks, and frequently are paid the least.

Yet women's substantial role in and contribution to agriculture remains invisible.

Their problems as pesticide sprayers – especially their health problems – are trivialized and rarely addressed. Although they may suffer ill effects due to pesticide exposure, many do not seek medical help; nor can they afford the luxury of consulting doctors or even local traditional health practitioners. In many countries women's subordinate positions in communities and families, their often low self esteem and their lack of knowledge of the hazards do not allow an expression or assertion of their rights and concerns for their well being.

The study

Due to the invisibility of the issue and lack of information on women and pesticide related problems, the Pesticide Action Network Asia and the Pacific (PAN AP) formulated a programme to provide information, publish resources in local languages and provide skills training on pesticide hazards. In the years 1991–1995, more than 2,500 farmers and agricultural workers, mostly women, were interviewed as a part of the research covering the impact of pesticides on women. The studies undertaken by network partners (national or local grassroots organizations) in Indonesia, Malaysia, Korea, Sri Lanka, Pakistan, the Philippines and India revealed the extent of the problem, and the extent of the invisibility and marginalization of women's problems with pesticide use.

Interviews with farmers formed the primary research, but analyses of published papers and statistics were also included. These studies will hopefully prompt additional research, specifically on epidemiological topics that would demonstrate the direct correlation between pesticide use and poisoning, and the adverse impact on women. The studies that have been carried out constitute a powerful tool for awareness building and training among farmers; they also help to garner support for alternatives – in particular, a move towards sustainable agriculture. Several results of the case studies can be stated.

- Most women farmers and workers interviewed sprayed pesticides or came in direct contact with pesticides in their work in other ways. In Malaysia, all of the plantation workers interviewed were pesticide sprayers.

- Farmers and agricultural workers in the region used highly toxic pesticides including methyl parathion and monocrotophos, as well as phorate and (in India) phosphamidon – all listed by the World Health Organization as Class 1 (extremely hazardous) pesticides.

- Most pesticide users interviewed were nevertheless unaware of the adverse effects of pesticides. In Malaysia, all of the women respondents stated they had received no training on how to properly mix and spray pesticides. In many cases, pesticide applicators could not read labels or did not follow instructions.

- Most users did not use protective clothing; it is unsuitable for the climate, unavailable or too expensive. Korea, where 53% of farmers surveyed said they used protective clothing, was the exception. However, in all seven countries where the survey was undertaken (not just in Korea) many farmers thought protective clothing meant a handkerchief over their face.

- Most of those surveyed stated they have been poisoned, citing acute effects such as dizziness, muscular pain, sneezing, itching, skin burns, blisters, difficulty in breathing, nausea, nails changing colour and/or sore eyes. Very few understood the specific adverse effects; most described ill effects in general or vague terms.

- Regarding disposal of leftover pesticides and containers, as shown in the case studies below, many of those interviewed in the Philippines left these in their own backyards or in an open field; some of the dangers this presents were exemplified by the children seen playing with used containers in Sri Lanka. The Pakistan study illustrated the domestic reuse of containers for spices, oil, food and medicine, giving pesticide residues an easy entrance into the body.

Before considering general conclusions, some results of the case studies conducted in four participating countries will be described.

Pakistan

In Pakistan, a two-year study was undertaken by Nasira Habib, Director of KHOJ Research and Publication, based in Lahore. The study was carried out as an initiative of PAN-AP's partner organization, KHOJ Research and Publication Centre, and a 130-page report, 'Invisible farmers in Pakistan – a Study on the Role of Women in Agriculture and the Impact of Pesticides on Them', was published (Habib, 1996). Conducted in seven rural villages in the district of Punjab-Rahim Yar Khan and including more than 210 interviews with farmers, the Pakistan Case Study findings are a clear example of how the pivotal role played by women in agriculture goes unrecognized. As Nasira points out, the problem of visible work–invisible workers has resulted in the further erosion of women's self image and marginalization of women's status in this fiercely patriarchal society (Habib, 1996). As a result of their socialization, women have come to perceive their own work as worthless: they devalue their own contribution to the overall domestic national product.

> *I came to the village after marriage. Did housework from morning to evening but to my sheer surprise my mother-in-law always told the visitors, 'she does not work'. Later it dawned on me that only those women are considered working who go out and work in the fields. (Woman interviewee cited by Habib, 1996)*

The experiential cases documented by the author show that when coupled with reproductive rearing and nurturing functions, women's work, including their contribution to agriculture, actually totals between 16 and 19 hours per day.

The official line

The study cites several definitions from the Pakistan Census of Agriculture of who or what constitutes an economically active worker or agricultural worker. The obsession with 'economic end product' or seeing women as 'part time workers' has meant their exclusion as full time workers. Women are categorized as 'housewives', or placed in other categories like 'economically inactive persons', hence delineating them as support rather than direct producers. 'This reflects the myopia of linking and equating the last service of marketing to profit and economic gain. This exclusion and denial of their work has led to women silently bearing the burden with no recognition', explains Nasira (Habib, 1996).

Furthermore, Nasira is unequivocal about the findings in relation to the effect of pesticide exposure on women:

> Women are affected adversely by pesticide use. They are exposed to the effects of toxic chemicals when working with seeds, in disposal and washing of containers, working in pesticide sprayed areas, picking cotton and so forth.

Exposure during pregnancy, inhalation of fumes and picking cotton in freshly sprayed areas ensure that frequency of pesticide exposure is high. As noted above, containers are reused domestically, enabling pesticide residues to enter the body through spices, oil, food and so forth as well. Medicines are also stored in pesticide containers. The study found that women complained of dizziness, muscular pain, cough, nausea, suffocation, blisters and acute pesticide poisoning due to inhalation of fumes. However, women's minimal access to health care, even in cases of visible discomfort, means there is no monitoring of the impact of pesticides on women's immune and reproductive systems (Habib, 1996).

Taking action

The study makes critical recommendations covering advocacy, research and mobilization vis-á-vis government agricultural policies and the role of the pesticide industry, as well as the role of NGOs and people's organizations, to counter the onslaught of pesticides in Pakistan. Gender sensitization and a focus on women in agriculture will require sensitive and integrated gender analysis, closing the information gap and stressing advocacy with respect to the effects of pesticides on women in particular but also the wider agricultural vista in general, and awareness-building initiatives about the alternatives. As Nasira states,

> To ensure women's participation in mainstream activities as equal partners, it is important that they emerge stronger. This envisages various inputs at different levels of society, and awareness mobilization activities to see women as individuals with the capacity for supporting society in all ways. Women's pivotal role in agriculture has to be analysed, discussed at all levels by academics and policymakers; this is to be backed by field data and research. It is only on the basis of various initiatives that women will emerge, still bearing burdens and working, but stronger and able to direct the forces that govern their lives. (Habib, 1996)

The Philippines

In the Philippines, a total of 952 households in ten villages in the municipality of Munoz were surveyed by community health workers between February and June, 1993. The surveyed communities use pesticides mainly in rice cultivation and to a smaller extent in vegetable farming. Of those interviewed, 532 respondents or 63.3% were women, and of these 93% sprayed pesticides. Fifty-nine per cent said they wore protective material, which usually consisted of a handkerchief over their face. In disposing of leftover pesticides and containers, 29% said they threw them in their own backyards; another 28% threw them in an open field. The most frequently used pesticides were reported to be butachlor (Machete), cypermethrin (Cymbush), monocrotophos (Nuvacron), and endosulfan (Thiodan).

When asked about the ill effects of pesticides, respondents stated pesticides cause illness, are bad for health or poison the body (31%), cause dizziness (23%) or cause death (14%). Very few understood the specific adverse effects; most described ill effects in general or vague terms. Most survey respondents said they used pesticides either 'too much' or 'much'. Estimated average annual expenditure per household ranged from about 800 pesos to 1,500 pesos – about 2.1 to 3.9% of the estimated average annual family income. Considering that only about 1.7% of annual family income goes to medical care and 2.9% to education, pesticide costs use up a relatively great proportion of the family's small income.

Sri Lanka

The study was undertaken by the Community Education Centre (CEC) in the early months of 1995. PAN AP's questionnaire was first revised by an agriculturist and then discussed and further revised by five animators working in the villages and the two members of CEC who carried out the survey. The 100 survey respondents were women farmers living in Matale and Anuradapura districts in Sri Lanka and planting paddy, tobacco, Bombay onions, chili and vegetables. None of the women owned the land they worked.

Pesticide exposure

Half of the women interviewed spray pesticides on crops; as many as 35% apply pesticides twice a week. They spray from around 90 minutes to as long as three hours in a stretch without a break. Of the 100 women interviewed only two used gloves when spraying. Most of them do not take any precautions, and some chew betel as they spray. Many were unable to read the instructions on the pesticide labels. About 15% of the women constantly suffer from headaches, giddiness and nausea when using pesticides. The women interviewed reported that about 16 women in the area have died due to pesticide poisoning.

Women continue caring for their children while working in the fields. Even during spraying operations, the children are in the vicinity; their mothers may carry them while applying pesticides, and women farmers breastfeed their children in the fields. Thus young children and babies are invariably exposed. Children are also seen playing with used pesticide containers, and in addition they often help their families carry the pesticides and store them in their homes.

Pesticides are frequently stored in the home along with grains, other crops and cooking utensils, as there is no other storage facility. After use, spray tanks are washed in the nearest river or stream – which is also used for bathing and for watering and bathing animals. Wells are not covered. Overall, the potential for contamination is very high. None of the women had undergone any training, although 4% had sought the advice of government extension officers. All of the women participating in the survey indicated they were very interested in knowing more about the hazards of pesticides and in seeking alternatives.

Malaysia

In Malaysia, 50 women participated in in-depth interviews carried out by Tenaganita, a local NGO, between January and June 1991. Of those interviewed, 100% were plantation workers who spray pesticides, all of whom reported suffering skin rash due to the use of paraquat. About 50% of the women surveyed said they suffered sore, red eyes and another 60% said they had discoloured, irregular nails. The survey showed a lack of washing facilities in the field where workers spray pesticides; workers seldom wash even when pesticides spill onto their skin. All those interviewed explained that even after four hours of spraying they were unable to wash until they returned home.

Workers also indicated they had received no training on how to properly mix and spray pesticides. One said: 'I use my bare hands to mix pesticides. I don't know if doing it is harmful to me in the long run. But I know it burns my skin.'

Planning the future: what next

Each of the studies conducted thus far has provided baseline information for discussions at national and local levels. Workshops have been conducted at these levels to discuss the problems and identify training needs and information gaps, as well as to plan efforts to address the problems. In designing the workshop sessions, PAN AP worked closely with its network partners. These are their recommendations:

- The problems with pesticide use demonstrated by the studies undertaken in these countries are a major cause of concern, especially since many of the chemicals in use are on the World Health Organization's list of extremely hazardous pesticides.

- The reality of life and conditions in rural Asia suggest that only a concerted effort will provide long-term solutions. A comprehensive policy to reduce pesticide use and dependence is needed, with clear proposals that will help farmers towards more sustainable approaches such as organic agriculture, which promote the use of alternative pest control strategies.

- If a more holistic and sustainable agriculture is to be promulgated, it will be crucial to recognize and value women's indispensable labour, skills and knowledge. We also need to learn from and build on women's knowledge of traditional alternative farming, using the tools and technologies of farmers who practice sustainable agriculture. (Women's knowledge is often more intact since they are less exposed to modern techniques; for example they have less often adopted high input green revolution technologies.) Learning, innovating and building on women's knowledge are integral aspects of promoting gender sensitive, appropriate and sustainable forms of agriculture. However, the invisibility of the role and contribution of women is pervasive in Asian societies. They are discriminated against; their position within the family and community is both subordinate and subservient. If women, who hold up half the sky and often contribute more than husbands and brothers, are to have their knowledge and work recognized as equal to that of men, then their contributions will have to be acknowledged and they will have to be empowered to assert their rights and their place in society.

- Women have raised their voices and struggled against such discrimination and will continue to do so. What is needed is both policy support and community support for these endeavours.

Conclusions

PAN AP's own purview with respect to the issue of women in agriculture is the primary need to tackle the invisibility and need for empowerment of rural women. Findings from the case studies briefly described above, workshops and feedback from PAN AP's Steering Council and 1994 Task Force on Women in Agriculture, as well as follow-up activities requested for the Women and Pesticides Programme, have helped to design the Women in Agriculture programme launched in 1995, much of which will continue until the year 2000. General objectives of the Programme include studying the impact of economic, technological, social and political trends on women farmers and agricultural workers. Also crucial will be the support and promotion directed towards the revival, adoption and implementation of sustainable agriculture, as well as efforts to build on the existing knowledge of women about sustainable agriculture. Plans for advocacy include identifying, developing and implementing strategies at national, regional and international levels to lead towards empowerment of women with respect to decision making. Specifically, the documentation of the impact of technologies on women in agriculture, particularly pesticides and bio-technology, will feature prominently. Plans are also afoot to bring together, edit and publish the overall findings from the seven-country case study on women and pesticides.

Note

1 Executive Director, Pesticide Action Network Asia and the Pacific.

Bibliography

Danish EPA, 'Male reproductive health and environmental chemicals with estrogenic effects'. Copenhagen, Ministry of Environment and Energy, Danish Environmental Protection Agency, 1995.

Habib, N., *Invisible farmers in Pakistan: a study on the role of women in agriculture and the impact of pesticides on them*. Penang, Malaysia, Pesticide Action Network Asia and the Pacific, 1996.

Hileman, B., 'Environmental estrogens linked to reproductive abnormalities, cancer'. *Chemical and Engineering News* (1994, January 31).

Jeyaratnam, J., 'Acute pesticide poisoning: a major global health problem'. *World Health Statistics Quarterly*, vol. 43 (1990).

Repetto, R. and S.S. Baliga, *Pesticides and the immune system: the public health risks*. Washington D.C., World Resources Institute, 1996.

Soto, A.M., 'Testimony before the Subcommittee on Health and the Environment', US House of Representatives, 21 October, 1993 (not published).

Sarah J. Tisch[1] and Natalia Poznanskaya[2]

2 Russian women's roles in crop protection in the new agricultural economy

Economic restructuring in the agricultural sector has stimulated fundamental changes in Russian agricultural production practices and in which individuals are involved. Two of the consequences are a decline in the use of chemical regimes for field crop protection, and a reduction in women's employment in the research and development of plant protection services - an area in which, within the former Soviet agroindustrial system, women used to be predominant.[1] Such changes in human capital inevitably impact agricultural production systems and thus the ability of a country to achieve food security. In Russia, ignoring the gender issues connected with this change in the use made of human capital can profoundly affect future agricultural productivity.

This could indicate, if there is a *gendered* linkage between the female capital base and agricultural productivity, that the current economic restructuring serves as an excuse to remove women from positions of responsibility. However, it is also plausible that while women dominated plant protection systems in the past, changes in women's employment and/or responsibilities reflect declines in agricultural employment by the state for both men and women. While fundamental research in other economies demonstrates the gendered nature of women's roles in agriculture (Heyzer, 1987; Poats, Schmink and Spring, 1988; Feldstein and Poats, 1989; Vidaver, 1988), these relationships have not yet received much attention in Russia. Research has shown, however, that female professionals have been among the first employees to lose their positions in former Soviet institutions as a result of economic restructuring (Khotkina, 1995).

In this chapter we first explore field crop protection practices for primary cereal field crops during the late Soviet period and the roles women played in the research and design, manufacture, management and application of these regimes. We then summarize more recent field crop protection practices based on eight case studies at privatized collective or state farms, and private farms. Alternative pest management methods are only vaguely beginning to appear on the horizon; this material makes clear some of the difficulties that will be faced in attempting to implement such changes. Nevertheless, the process may create new opportunities for women.

Field crop protection in Russia

From 1980–1985, the estimated total grain loss in the USSR from weeds, diseases and insect pests was about 14–17 million tonnes per year, with contributions of 6.0, 8.4 and 10.6%, respectively, from each of these three factors (Melnikov, 1987). Of the total grain output of 180–225 million tonnes, about 17–18 million tonnes of affected grain were estimated to have been saved through use of pesticides (Fadeev et al., 1988). Between 1986 and 1990 total annual grain losses in the Russian Federation were about

26.1 million tonnes, or 25% of the total annual grain output of about 104 million tonnes (Zaharenko and Zaharenko, 1995). Currently, the yield, quality and total output of grain in Russia do not meet the domestic demand for human consumption and animal feed.

About 25% of total grain losses are attributed to weed proliferation (Zaharenko and Zaharenko, 1995); the 1987 USSR crop survey also indicated moderate to severe levels of weed infestation. It is estimated that effective mechanical and chemical weed control would increase grain crop yields by 9 to 18% (Zaharenko, 1994). Diseases are another threat: more than 20 harmful diseases – smut, mildew, root rotting, snow mold, spur, leaf and stem rust and fusarium, among others – infect cereal crops in various regions of Russia. Chemical seed treatment is one of the critical factors in protecting grain crops, and is considered the most ecologically safe and inexpensive preventative technique. Insect pests have clearly also been a major threat.

Government and scientists have responded to these problems by developing and distributing a variety of plant protection chemicals, which contributed to dramatic increases in agricultural production (although their long-term environmental impact is unknown). For instance, during the 1980s the USSR was first in fertilizer production, and by 1985 was the eighth largest producer of pesticides in the world (Ovchinnikov, 1988). Today, significantly fewer types of pesticides are available in Russia and other parts of the former USSR than in other countries. Farmers are using both Russian and imported chemicals, and the expansion of a market environment is likely to increase the variety in types of pesticides available to farms. However, declines in production of chemicals and equipment for application, as well as in organizations providing practical and scientific agrochemical services to collective/ state farms and on-farm agrochemical departments, are central problems for conventional plant protection. This situation is compounded by losses in pesticide-related jobs, particularly for trained women.

Russian women's roles in agricultural sectors

Rural changes

Women and their roles in agriculture must be seen against the background of political, social, economic, and demographic problems in rural areas that particularly affect women. The most significant change is the reorganization of collective and state farms. By 1995 more than 24 thousand collective and state farms – about 95% of the total – had been privatized and re-registered (Shatalov, 1994; Terent'ev, 1995). These bodies (which have primarily become joint stock associations) continue to hold most of the land. However this property is still not held privately by individuals and generally may not be used as collateral. New private farms are set up each year, but many fail; Fedorova (1993) notes this is often because the farmer's wife wants to quit farming. Many rural women work as labourers in agriculture and plant protection; growing unemployment among rural women cannot help but have a significant impact on yields and quality. In different regions 70 to 91% of all registered farm owners are men (Bogdanovskii, 1993; Bondarenko and Ladenkov, 1993). Few women are officially registered as private farmers, although in fact they may be managing the farm.

Higher education in agriculture

As in other areas of the world, women have always played a critical and visible role in Russian agriculture (Sorokin and Nazarochkina, 1994; Es'kin et al., 1979; Pankov, 1979; Kudryashov and Shoklina, 1992). Yet as Dolgova noted in 1902, in spite of their many roles in agriculture, until 1900 there was no state agricultural school providing higher education for women, and only three private lower schools taught agricultural and housekeeping skills. By 1902, however, there were fourteen private women's agricultural schools. Whatever the shortcomings of this education may have been, the importance of having a technically educated female population working in agriculture was recognized by the private and public sector, and this continued throughout the Soviet period. In 1965–1985, about 50% of students in higher education (college or university) were women, as were about 40% of students at technical schools for industry and transportation and for about 30% in agriculture. Secondary schools percentages were similar (40% and 37% respectively; Narodnoye hozaistvo, 1922–1982). In 1989, 60% of those with higher education were women, and of these 45% had degrees in agronomy, livestock production or veterinary science (Gomskomstat, 1989).

Chemical production

During the Soviet period, women dominated the field of plant protection, taking part in every stage of research and design from synthesis of new biologically active compounds to pesticide production and physical appli-cation in fields. Between 1985 and 1990 the number of scientists and scientific technicians declined by about 11%; this trend appears to be continuing as a result of economic restructuring (Gohberg and Mindelli, 1994).

In Russia, scientific research is conducted in the member institutes of the Russian Academy of Agricultural Science; research on the effect of pesticides on human health are the domain of the Ministry of Health. The Scientific Research Institute for Plant Protection Chemicals, established in 1963 and located in Moscow, is the key institute for developing new plant protection chemicals and policy. Despite its premier position, the Institute is plagued by the same loss of scientists affecting all Russian research institutes: with the crisis besetting the Russian economy and the loss of advantages once associated with scientific work, both male and female scientists are leaving for better-paying jobs in other fields or other countries. There has been a three-fold decrease in staff since 1985, particularly among the mostly highly qualified female scientists, who have made up most of its staff.

While difficult to obtain, we did also find data from one of the more famous chemical plants built during the Soviet period, *Pervomajskoe gosudarstvenno predprijatie* or 'Himprom,' located in Ukraine, near the current Russian border. The plant produces a wide spectrum of chemicals for agricultural and industrial use, including herbicides, insecticides, fungicides, and seed coaters. This plant was one of the main suppliers to the former Soviet agroindustrial complex, and is still an important supplier in Russia. Women, who dominated the plant at all levels in the last Soviet years, now comprise fewer than half of the workforce. They are now primarily laboratory assistants, doing analysis or preparations for analysis or other laboratory work. Administrative and professional (scientific degree) staff positions are now primarily occupied by men, whereas during Soviet times these positions were held by women. Women – from professional scientists to administrators – were the first to be laid off when the Soviet Union collapsed. These women have found it virtually impossible to find similar scientific or administrative positions in the area; many have tried to find jobs in small-scale retail businesses or the service sector.

Rural women in plant protection

Rural women have played an enormous role in agriculture in Russia as in other countries (Bestujev-Lada, 1992; Dunn, 1980). However, many researchers note that consistent information on their status is still difficult to obtain in Russia, especially because of the well-known problems of data from the Soviet period.

In 1989, 34% of all women in Russia were rural dwellers (Bestujev-Lada, 1992). In 1980–1992, 53% of Russian women were employed; approximately 40% worked in agriculture, with about half in scientific jobs. In contrast, rural women have comparatively less education and tend to work at physical labour. According to the 1975 census, about 81% of rural women were working as hand labourers, most in crop production. However, Nikolaeva (1977) provides the best information on unskilled female labour. She analysed data from 60 farms, with a total of 5808 female workers as interviewees. By profession, Nikolaeva found 52.9% of women working as unskilled labourers and 42.3% as semi-skilled labourers. Most significantly, she reports that more than 66.6% of female labourers worked with pesticides. Pankov (1979) indicates that about 80% of female collective farm workers are engaged in crop production, with a predominance of women working in the physical preparation of plant protection chemicals or application to crops. On state and collective farms, despite a fairly high percentage of female specialists, there is an unjustified division between male and female labour: men tend to operate machines, while women perform physical labour not involving machinery.

These studies indicate the extent to which Russian women are involved with agricultural production, and particularly with the associated physical labour. However, women's decision making responsibilities related to pesticide production and use has declined sharply since the Soviet period. We believe this sharp decrease reflects a gender division of labour in Russian agriculture, where women in professional scientific or management positions are being replaced by men, while women can now most easily find jobs as physical labourers.

Plant protection and gender issues on Russian farms

To learn more about rural women's current involvement in crop protection, we conducted case studies on eight farms – four privatizing former state farms and four private farms that had never been a part of a state or collective farm[1]. Such farms typically include male and female labourers from families that have been on the farm for more than one generation (unless the farm was established during the last few years of the Soviet Union); collective or state farm workers had little mobility, since movement was controlled by the Communist Party or the farm director. For both men and women, education (e.g. academic excellence) or Party loyalty were what provided opportunities to leave the farm.

On former state farms, farm directors, agronomists and agricultural workers were interviewed; on private farms family members were interviewed. The results illustrate the diversity of cereal production in Russia today and the lack of access farms have to pesticides. However, the summary of conditions provides examples, which are not meant to be taken as representing the diversity found on Russian farms in total.

State farms

All state farms visited are located in central Russia, where part of Ryazan and all of the Rostov region fall within the black earth or chernozem zone, the most fertile soils of Russia. At one time all of these state farms had a plant protection specialist, but this person had either left due to lack of pay and materials or was not using any chemical means of plant protection because either chemicals or cash to purchase them were not available. Few farms now use pesticides, and yields have significantly declined due to disease and weeds; alternative methods of pest and weed management are rarely known or practised. As a result, more land is being taken out of production each season. Such effects are not obvious now, but if the situation continues it is hard to believe grain yields even on the remaining land will not be affected, since neither pesticides nor information on mechanical means of plant protection are available. Thus these farms are likely to continue to produce grain at current or declining rates. The situation on this large group of farms is ripe for alternative (nonchemical) means of pest and weed control, but money and opportunities for information/training are also lacking.

Private farms

Private farms in Russia are generally resource constrained, with little access to credit. These farms were never part of a former collective or state farm. Farmers obtained land by applying to local level officials under various land distribution programs. The most successful farmers either focus on subsistence farming or have developed special market niches for their products, such as goats, bees, dairy products or pigs. Very few private farms compete with former collective or state farms in grain production (Kuetsev, 1992; Wegren, 1992; Brooks and Lerman, 1994; Epshtein, 1993).

Most private farms of this nature are family farms, with worker/owners comprising an extended family. Old and young, men and women all contribute to farm production. Private farms depend upon locally available resources and the goodwill of local officials and former collective/state farm directors for assistance and advice (Kalugina, 1991). Private farmers often have their own unique ideas about farming practices.

The private farmers we spoke with are not using pesticides. While all the farms we visited recognized their effectiveness, they could not afford pesticides, could not obtain them or had philosophical reasons for not using them. Organic farming techniques were used instead, with knowledge gained from Western periodicals. Crop problems that necessitate use of pesticides have not yet been experienced. Other than through specialists on local state/collective farms and information they seek out on their own initiative, these farmers have little access to information about crop production or protection, including pesticide regimes used in Russia. However, in fact most private farmers concentrate on livestock production because the returns on their investment are greater.

Conclusion

Our case studies of eight farms indicate that the former system of plant protection is no longer within the reach of newly privatized state and collective farms. In most places pesticide availability is less of a problem than inability to pay. The lack of a competitive market, reliable private producers and dealers in plant protection chemicals, as well as a farm credit system, are central problems for both newly privatized state and collective farms and private farms. Additionally, without heavily subsidizing the sector, it is unclear how the government will be able to continue research and development of pesticide regimes. Thus in the short run, field crops yields are definitely at risk in comparison to the past. Yields are declining, but more importantly diseases and weeds are spreading. These are far more difficult to control once they have reached epidemic levels, and unless alternative methods are introduced will require an even heavier use of plant protection chemicals than in the past.

Farms, and in particular private farms, are using biological or mechanical means for plant protection. This can be viewed as a positive attempt to achieve sustainable agriculture. However, it is unclear whether these methods provide a viable alternative for the larger farms that are still the major suppliers of Russia's grain needs. To encourage change, the introduction of new, nonchemical methods would require a concerted campaign in the popular media and discussions at all levels. Given the preeminent position that women once played in the chemically oriented field of plant protection, this could create opportunities for women to once again take leadership in Russian agriculture. A female scientific and technical workforce still exists, which could be retrained to adapt and popularize alternative or sustainable agriculture methods that will combat disease and pests and produce decent yields.

While we have outlined the fundamental roles women play in the Russian agricultural sector, including their roles in plant protection from the scientific research institute to the private farm, the data and research reported here make clear that at present Russian women are leaving the field of plant protection. The data available do not allow us to assert that their reasons are related to a preference of employers to retain male rather than female workers. However, people with whom we spoke all indicated this is an increasing trend.

Female agricultural workers are leaving the farms for economic reasons, as female scientists are leaving institutes for the same reasons – they have either not been paid the wages they need to support their families or their jobs have literally vanished. It is clear that the incentive system used to reward workers on newly privatized farms is also unacceptable for unskilled female labourers – they have little job mobility and are paid much lower wages for the same work than their male counterparts. Why more women than men are now farm labourers remains a question. This is also related to a larger question concerning changes in gender relations since the dissolution of the former USSR. Recent research in the Orlov region indicates women have lost status and access to the property rights that were available to them under the old system. This decline in women's claims to rights is having a critical effect on the status of rural women (Krestiyanskye vedomosti, 1995). However, the extent to which women could really exercise their rights within state and collective farms in the old system is also unknown.

For women who have lost their employment in plant protection and who are not scientists, the alternatives according to many Russian sociologists are small subsistence farms or housekeeping. Women thus are leaving active economic life in agriculture; they have few options and are returning to the home. The effect on household income of this withdrawal of women from the formal agricultural economy needs to be examined. Some female scientists are finding other, perhaps less satisfying, employment but not all have found alternatives. Special courses for retooling are perhaps needed, but until the direction of the Russian economy becomes clearer, it is hard to discern useful skills that can be learned given minimal resources. Nevertheless, a new system must emerge to allow research on and development of methods of plant protection in Russia. Recognition of the role played by women in this field provides a base from which a new, more responsive system can be developed that will serve the needs of both smaller private farms and larger privatized state farms.

Notes

1 Winrock International Institute for Agricultural Development, Morrilton, Arkansas, USA.
2 Scientific Research Institute for Plant Protection Chemicals, Moscow, Russia.
3 The authors are grateful to Winrock International Institute for Agricultural Development for research support and travel funds for Tisch, and the John D. and Catherine T. MacArthur Foundation for providing travel funds for Poznanskaya. For the ideas we present, however, we take full responsibility; this should not be attributed to any of those who have helped us.
4 These farms were selected from a group of 80 agroenterprises that have received technical assistance through the US Agency for International development-funded project, NIS Farmer-to-Farmer (1993–1996), Russia, implemented by Winrock International Institute for Agricultural Development.

Bibliography

Bestujev-Lada, J., 'Are there women in Russian villages?' *Hozjain*, vol. 1 (1992), pp. 43–45.
Bogdanovskii, Y.A., Social-labor potential. In: *Social problems of farm development in nonblack soil zone*. St. Petersberg, Rossiikoi Federatsii sbornik naughnyh trudov, 1993.
Bondarenko L.B. and N.V. Ladenkov, 'Social-economic problems of farm development in Nijnegorodsaya region'. In: *Social problems of farm development in nonblack soil zone*. St. Petersberg, Rossiikoi Federatsii sbornik naughnyh trudov, 1993.
Brooks K. and Z. Lerman, 'Land reform and farm restructuring in Russia'. World Bank Discussion Papers, no. 233. Washington, D.C., World Bank, 1994.
Dolgova, N., *Women's role in agriculture*. St. Petersberg, Volf, Tpl.1902.
Dunn, E., 'Factors affecting social mobility for women in the Soviet countryside'. In: *Agricultural policies in the USSR and Eastern Europe*. Boulder, CO, Westview Press, 1980.
Epshtein, D., *The cooperative movement in the Soviet Union: history and future prospects*. Boulder, CO, Westview Press, 1993.
Es'kin, P.I., N.B. Gorbachev and G.P. Baldin, 'Labor protection of women in agriculture'. *Rossel'khozizdat*, vol. 54 (1979), no.1.

Fadeev, Y.N., K.V. Novojilov and S.L. Tuterev, *Zhurnal Vsesousnogo Himicheskogo im. Mendeleeva*, XXIII (1988), no. 6, pp. 613–618.

Fedorova, G.P., 'Development of peasants-owner farms and reasons for their activity interruption'. In: *Social problems of farm development in nonblack soil zone*. St. Petersberg, Rossiikoi Federatsii sbornik naughnyh trudov, 1993.

Feldstein, H.S. and S.V. Poats, eds., *Working together: gender farming systems research and extension*. Boulder, CO, Westview Press, 1989.

Gohberg L.M. and L.E. Mindelli, *Novaya Rossia*. Moscow, Mezhdunarodnaia Akameniia Informatizatzii, 1994, pp. 578–592.

Gomskomstat, *Zhenshiny in SSSR*. Moscow, Gomskomstat SSSR, 1989.

Heyzer, N., ed., *Women farmers and rural change in Asia: towards equal access and participation*. Kuala Lampur, Asian and Pacific Development Centre, 1987.

Kalugina, Z.I., 'Social constraints on developing peasant farms'. *Izvestiya Sibirskogo Oteleniya Akademii Nuak SSSR*, vol. 3 (1991), pp. 35–42.

Khotkina, Z., 'Gender aspects of unemployment and the system of social security'. Moscow, Human Right's Women's Project, 1995.

'The hard plight of women peasants'. *Krestiyanskye vedomosti*, nos. 17–18, p. 13 (1995).

Krusmetia N.R. and B.A. Rivja,. 'Employment of women-specialists in agricultural production of Latiiskou SSR'. *Izvestia AN, Latvia SSR*, 5 (466), (1986), pp. 93–90.

Kudryashov, V.I. and Z.N. Shoklina, 'Manpower requirements for animal husbandry products in private holdings attached to collective farms'. *Zootekhniya*, vol. 5/6 (1992), pp. 41–43.

Kuetsev, I., 'Organization and economic conditions for developing peasant farms'. *Ekonomika Upravlenie*, vol. 4 (1992), pp. 19–22.

Melnikov, N.N., 'Pesticidy'. Moscow, *Himiya*, vol. 11 (1987), pp. 711–713.

Narodnoye hozaistvo, SSSR., 1922–1982, 1990, 1991. 'Finansy i statistika'. Ubileinyi statisticheskiy sborni. Moscow, pp. 410, 452, 650.

Nikolaeva, A.V., 'Problems of women labor use in agriculture'. In: *Aktual'nye problemy truda sel'skom hozaistve, Sbornik nauchnykh trudov*. Moscow, M. NLLTruda, 1977.

Ovchinnikov, V., 'Pesticides, today and tomorrow'. *Zhurnal Vsesouznogo Himicheskogo, obchestva im. D.J. Mendeleeva*, vol. 33, no. 6 (1988), p. 609.

Pankov, G.M., *Women-machine operators*. Moscow, Rossel'khozizdat, 1979.

Poats, S.V., M. Schmink and A. Spring (eds.), *Gender analysis in agriculture*. Westport, CN, Kumarian Press, 1988.

Prokopov, F.T., 'Employment problems in transitional period'. In: *Novaya Rossiya*. Moscow, Mezhdunarodnaia Akameniia Informatizatzii, 1994.

Shatalov, S.M., 'Agrarian reform'. In: *Novaya Rossiya*, Moscow, Mezhdunarodnaia Akameniia Informatizatzii, 1994.

Sorokin, A.P. and E.V. Nazarochkina, Concentration and use of the labor force in collective farms of the non-black earth zone of the Russian Federal SSR. Sbornik Nauchnykh Trudov VNIESH Nauchno Izdatelstvo, vol. 71 (1994), pp. 165–173.

Terent'ev, T., 'The general results of work of agroindustrial complex in 1994'. *Ekonomist*, vol. 4 (1995), pp. 51–65.

Vidaver, A.K., 'Women in plant pathology: an assessment'. *Phytopathology*, vol. 78, no. 1 (1988), pp. 27–31.

Wegren, S.K., 'Private farming and agrarian reform in Russia'. *Problems of Communism*, vol. 41, no. 3 (1992), pp. 107–121.

Zaharenko, V.A. and A.V. Zaharenko, *Zashita rastenni*, vol. 3 (1995), pp. 6–7.

Zaharenko V.A., *Gerbicidy*, Moscow, V.O. Agropromisgatu, 1994.

Alida A. Laurense[1] and Fadhila H. Ali[2]

3 Women in plant protection in Zanzibar

Most agriculture in Zanzibar, as in much of Africa, is subsistence agriculture. In both male and female headed households, women are the main producers of food crops, and more than 60% of field activities are carried out by women. Further, it is a woman's responsibility to ensure that her family has enough to eat for the day. This is especially so where there are co-wives and a husband who cannot provide for all of their households. Any problems that affect food production therefore have a direct impact on the livelihood of women and children, and any impact of IPM strategies on the farming community will directly affect them.

On the other hand, there are no women extension officers at village level. The very few women extension officers (working at other levels as researchers or managers) have seldom grown up in a rural area, and typically have very little practical experience in agriculture when they start their jobs. Hence there is a gap between the farmers, who are mainly illiterate to semi-literate, and those who give advice, design programmes or conduct research. The objective of this paper is to look at all of these women and their relation to plant protection, and at ways different IPM strategies could be effectively implemented. In many cases no hard data is available, but some years of working in this area have provided consistent observations that have led to the picture and conclusions given here.

The farmer

Many African farmers are very poorly educated. In Tanzania, for example, although primary education has been compulsory and free for some 30 years the rural population has benefited very little. Women, especially the rural elderly, are generally the most disadvantaged, and have received little or no education. Even among the younger generation, for whom enrolment of boys and girls is almost equal at primary level, girls' participation in secondary school declines. An occasional farmer may have had a secondary education, but most such cases are retired male civil servants involved part time in agriculture.

Agriculture is officially part of the curriculum in the last years of primary school, but this consists mainly of manual work in the field, which therefore does not have much impact. No agricultural training is included in the three-year lower secondary education programme. The only training in agriculture and plant protection farmers receive comes through sessions organized by the Extension Service of the Ministry of Agriculture, or from related projects. Unless there is a specific request, however, these sessions are primarily attended by men. Even when women are present, they participate less actively than men. In some parts of Tanzanian society women lack the confidence to talk in the presence of men or male relatives. Hence questions are not openly discussed, which can lead to misinterpretation of information or advice given to farmers.

On-farm trials tend to be carried out by 'progressive' farmers, who are always men. Women are typically involved only in subsistence farming, since they own very little or no land and have no capital and/or power to make decisions. A married woman must leave decisions to the husband, and a single woman to her male relatives. Property inheritance rules do not favour women's obtaining land. Usually a woman inherits land or trees from parents, but her share is half that of a brother. It may be so small that she relinquishes the right to inherit or leaves its supervision to her brothers (Donkerlo and Kibao, 1994). All of this means women farmers have less contact with extension agents and therefore very little exposure to any innovations. They also have less 'spare' time to invest in such activities. As a result of these factors, men farmers are generally more eager to learn and, for example, to take part in trials related to innovations, than women; men own land, may have some capital and are able to invest in innovations that require additional knowledge and training.

These constraints on women's participation are recognized by farmers, governments and donors, but little has been done to alleviate them. Encouraging women to obtain more education could be a plausible long-term solution, as it could help to build up their confidence, thereby increasing the level of participation in programmes related to agriculture. In the short term, agricultural training and extension are very much needed.

Plant protection has been, and in many countries still is, synonymous with the promotion and use of pesticides. Because their use requires capital investments and an economic return to recover these costs, pesticides are typically only used on cash crops. This type of agriculture is dominated by men; women are only involved as 'labourers'. Consequently, technical knowledge of pests and diseases, pesticides and the skills to apply them has been transferred to men farmers, but not to women. Even when a female farmer decides to apply pesticides to her crop, she will often call on a trained man to do the job. A knapsack sprayer is an uncomfortably heavy load on a woman's back (women in Tanzania carry heavy loads, but on their heads!) and does not accord with the usual clothing of most rural women. This 'natural' resistance of women to applying pesticides could actually be seen as positive, considering the potential effect of pesticide application during pregnancy and lactation. An IPM strategy could benefit women farmers and encourage them not to use pesticides because:
- when properly followed, low financial investment is required;
- close monitoring of the crop is needed, to provide a basis for management decisions. This is relatively easily incorporated in women's activities: they are already often in the fields, weeding, thinning and pruning. It is also an activity which can be programmed into the time schedule of women;
- where natural, locally produced pesticides are included in the IPM strategy, preparation – e.g. crushing neem seeds or leaves in a mortar – is often a home activity.

However, if IPM is to be a management strategy that is suitable for women farmers, high priority should be given to including them in training and extension programmes. This is especially important, given that women are the main cultivators of food crops. However, it requires first sensitizing male extension workers; otherwise the selection of participants will result in the typically low percentage of women invited for training.

Even where the programme involves a traditional men's crop, women should be encouraged to attend – most likely the bulk of the work in these 'men's crops' is done by women anyway! But also, women can apply the methodology and principles learned in IPM training to other crops. Further, women can apply the methodology and principles learned in IPM training to their own crops.

When women are included, several points need to be kept in mind. During extension training activities, it has been observed that women are more confident, open and expressive in all-women groups than in mixed groups. This effect is even stronger when the facilitator is a woman. When female farmers are to be approached individually, a female extension worker may be the only workable solution; male extension workers are often not allowed to talk with an individual female farmer alone.

The extension agent

In Africa, agricultural extension is dominated by men. In Zanzibar, not one of the 97 village extension workers is female, nor is any district or regional extension officer. The only section within the extension service of the Ministry with a high number of women is the one dealing with Women and Youth! The two Extension (Field Service) Sections of the Plant Protection Division have an 'exceptionally' high number of female staff: 4 out of 15 are women (KAP Survey, 1995).

The underlying problem is the low level of education of girls. To be an extension agent requires a certificate in agriculture, for which one must have completed at least secondary education. In rural areas there are extremely few and sometimes no qualified girls. In urban schools the situation is slightly better, although the percentage of girls is also low. Data from the Ministry of Education (1992–1994) show that a total of 30% of those who have completed primary school enter high school (and therefore after two years can qualify to enter any diploma course). Only one or two of these town girls per year opt for further education in agriculture.

Once women have a certificate and are employed by the Ministry of Agriculture, they like their male counterparts are interested in going further, that is, in a diploma and related courses. However, family obligations after marriage may discourage woman from continuing their education. And if selected, most girls are only given a chance if they take a course in nutrition, since the places in agriculture and horticulture tend to be filled by their male colleagues. This is quite unfortunate if we consider the advantages a female extension agent has in reaching women farmers. She is more free to interact with these women, and usually has a better eye for their special needs.

When a woman does manage to become an extension agent, to do her job well she will need to be able to cope with several factors:
• she will have to be better (more knowledgeable, confident, punctual and hard working) than her male counterpart to be accepted, especially by male farmers;
• she will have to be mobile. Normally motorbikes are provided for this purpose, but their use poses several problems for female agents. There are social restrictions on riding a motorbike (many husbands oppose it); women are afraid of technical breakdowns, which may leave them alone in the bush; they experience harassment from passers-by; and during pregnancy, motorbike trips on rough bush tracks are not advisable;
• she will need to find a way to deal with field activities, which may require overnight camping. Married women are sometimes not allowed by their husbands to take part, or only allowed if other women are present.

To increase the number of female extension agents, the following steps should be taken.

- Use both non-formal and formal training to make the most of the potential of rural women: semi-literate, intelligent and assertive women can be found in every village. They are eager to learn and to extend their knowledge, but have never had a chance to fully develop their skills. In most cases they are leaders of the women's groups that deal with various income generating activities. They could be trained to become village extension workers in areas such as those related to IPM.

- Draw on the potential of the rural areas for the future:
  - encourage girls to complete primary and secondary education. Those with qualifications could be given priority for training in agriculture;
  - make agriculture an attractive activity, which can provide a respectable income and status. Agricultural activities at school should not be a punishment but a useful and important part of the curriculum;
  - look for ways to make being an agricultural extension agent an attractive alternative to the traditional women's jobs of teacher, nurse or secretary.

Further, women who are now extension officers could be encouraged to develop their careers, for example by becoming a trainer of trainers or specializing, perhaps in IPM.

The researcher

The constraints discussed above spill over, resulting in very low enrolment of women in agricultural undergraduate courses. University education is generally only possible when one has secured a scholarship awarded by the local government or by donors, through the fellowship programmes within projects. In many instances, donor scholarships are only offered for MSc courses; some of these are very short, superficial and not actually relevant to the research demands encountered in the home country. Obtaining a scholarship for further studies after a BSc depends very much on the initiative of the potential candidate, whether male or female. Both also experience the inconvenience of being dependent on outside financing to plan their studies. Obtaining project approval, waiting for funding and securing admission to a university or college can cause considerable delay. This can be difficult for either a man or a woman who intends to start a family, but is more problematic for women, since there is a specific age range in which they can start a family.

Two-thirds of agricultural researchers in Tanzania are men. However, it is interesting to note that on the Tanzania mainland, equal numbers of men and women are plant pathologists, while this is not the case for entomologists (SACCAR Directory, 1993). In Zanzibar, women plant pathologists even outnumber men by three to two. Could this be due to the nature of the work and a preference of women with respect to their choice of a field of study? Whatever the reason, more female researchers tend to work in laboratories and carry out on-station trials, whereas their male colleagues have more contact with farmers in on-farm activities.

Universities tend to be male strongholds. In 1993 at the Sokoine University of Agriculture (SUA) in Morogoro, Tanzania, for example, the Department of Crop Science and Production responsible for courses in plant protection, of 27 members of the academic staff only three were female, although the head of department was one of them. What are the career prospects for a researcher in plant protection? These include:

- head of a (research) division or department;
- administrator/senior administrator in the government system;
- university lecturer/university professor;
- technical expert in an international organization/institute;
- director general of an international organization/institute.

Obviously the number of women in the higher posts is negligible. However, if they were to be encouraged to apply for such research posts, and were given equal opportunity in competing for a post, this situation could be reversed.

The policymaker

Women plant protection graduates are scarcely represented at management and policymaking levels. This is reflected in the government as a whole at all levels (Table 1) – where decisions are made regarding agriculture or the status of women in general. Is this a disadvantage? And is female representation a must? We think it is. There are no reasons for women not to be represented equally in all positions. Even though the number of qualified women is limited, a sufficient number are available. Although this may sound questionable in the present situation, we are convinced that the ability to acquire and use technical knowledge is gender independent. However, with respect to communication, working relations and efficiency in management, gender related issues are crucial. Another positive aspect of having women policy-makers present is their awareness of the needs of women staff and farmers.

Table 1 Women in policymaking positions

Position	1985-1990	% of total	1991-1995	% of total
Minister	2	18.0	3	19.0
Deputy Minister	0	0	1	17.0
Principal Secretary	0	0	0	0
Director	5	10.0	5	10.0
Regional Commissioner	0	0	0	0
District Commissioner	0	0	0	0
House Representative	11	15.0	11	15.0

Source: Ministry of Women and Children's Affairs, 1998

In many instances women receive less encouragement to apply for managerial posts than their male colleagues. It is important to note that the training and experience that help one to prepare for such posts are more readily offered to men than to women. Further, the first ten to fifteen years of a career, when the foundations for a future executive job are laid, coincide with the time when most women have the double role of being an employee and a mother. This leaves them with little time to attend additional courses or maintain long working hours (over 60 hours a week) as is generally 'required' by executive jobs. Unfortunately, skills acquired in managing a household are not considered when applying for a managerial position.

Resistance to a woman's working towards a career that could lead to a higher-level job often comes from her own family, and indirectly from the woman herself. The family fears she will neglect her family duties and obligations and perhaps surpass her husband in knowledge level, skills and salary. Against all odds, a few women have made their way up and hold respectable positions, although it is a general belief that such a woman could never have achieved the position on her own. She must have been somebody's girlfriend, who has 'bought' her way up by using her 'feminine skills'. This belief is so deeply rooted that some bosses are afraid of promoting women, and women may be afraid to apply for higher positions for fear of gossip, suspicion and 'getting a bad name'.

Conclusions

Women in the categories discussed have some common problems in relation to the implementation of an IPM programme: they tend to be left out of training programmes; issues covered in training are not relevant to their jobs or crops; and they carry out less-responsible jobs or activities than men. Gender sensitization – especially where men are the decision makers – seems to be the main solution; both men and women should be aware of the roles played by the other in agriculture and life in general. When a participatory approach is used, with researchers and farmers acting as equal participants, IPM strategies will be more successful. Women should receive more emphasis because they are the major producers of food for their families. To achieve this will require increasing the number of women extension agents in particular, but also of researchers and policymakers. It is especially important for women in senior management positions not to alienate themselves from other women, as they can have great influence on the planning and implementation of programmes related to both agriculture and farm life in general.

Notes

1 Plant Protection Division, Ministry of Agriculture, Livestock and Natural Resources, P. O. Box 1062, Zanzibar, Tanzania
2 Commission for Research and Extension, Ministry of Agriculture, Livestock and Natural Resources, P.O. Box 159, Zanzibar, Tanzania

Bibliography

Ali, F.H., A.I. Khatibu and M.A. Foum, *Survey of farmers: Knowledge, Attitude and Practices (KAP) on five food crops and poultry production for a strategic extension campaign in Zanzibar*, The United Republic of Tanzania, 1995.
Donkerlo, J. and A.A. Kibao, 'Women and land in Zanzibar'. Report prepared by Zanzibar Enterprise Development Organisation (ZEDO), 1994.
Ministry of Education, Zanzibar, 'Hotuba ya Waziri wa Elimu Mheshimiwa Omar. R. Mapuri Kuhusu Mapato na Makadirio ya Mapato na Makadirio ya Mapato na Matumizi ya Fedha wa Wizara ya Elimuy Kwa Mwaka 1998/99'. (Ministry of Education's 1995/96 budget speech, June 1995.)
Ministry of Education, Zanzibar, 'Hotuba ya Waziri wa Elimu Mheshimiwa Omar. R. Mapuri Kuhusu Mapato na Makadirio ya Mapato na Makadirio ya Mapato na Matumizi ya Fedha wa Wizara ya Elimuy Kwa Mwaka 1994/95'. (Ministry of Education's 1994/95 budget speech, June 1994.)Ministry of Education, Zanzibar, 'Hotuba ya Waziri wa Elimu Mheshimiwa Omar. R. Mapuri Kuhusu Mapato na

Makadirio ya Mapato na Makadirio ya Mapato na Matumizi ya Fedha wa Wizara ya Elimuy Kwa Mwaka 1993/94'. (Ministry of Education's 1993/94 budget speech, June 1993.)

Ministry of Women and Children's Affairs, 'Takwimu za Wanawaka katika shughuli mbali mbali za uongozi na maendeleo Zanzibar, November 1998', 1998.

SACCAR, *SACCAR Directory, 1993*, Southern African Center for Cooperation in Agricultural and Natural Resources Research and Training (SACCAR), Gaborone, 1993.

B.J. Vander Mey[1]

4 Establishing gender sensitive IPM:
a cowpea programme in Ghana

Women have been routinely pushed or left out of development programs in the past; the exclusion of women's realities and women's roles in farm families and farm market systems of developing countries has been well documented. The costs for women, their families and their countries are probably incalculable. In addition to problems discussed in other chapters, such as the tendency to exclude women farmers' realities and roles when developing projects or to give low priority to extension outreach to women, structural adjustment programs (SAPs) have also had major effects. Preliminary research documents that women in Africa disproportionately bore the costs of such programs during the 1980s – costs including less educational attainment, difficulty in securing employment, and poor health/ limited access to health care (Beckley, 1993; Vander Mey, 1995). In Ghana, SAPs also tended to disproportionately burden women (Brydon and Legge, as reviewed by Chalfin, 1997). Moreover, evidence is clear that as implemented in Ghana, they alienated farmers and market women (Kraus, 1991). And, in Ghana, at least 50% of the women are farmers.

On the other hand, 'the important role of women in development has been recognized by international agencies and national governments throughout sub-Saharan Africa' (Barrett and Browne, 1991, p. 242). But while gender bias in structural adjustment programs is being addressed, criticism remains regarding how the 'woman question' is treated. For instance, some researchers (e.g., Blumberg, 1989) emphasize the 'internal economy of the household.' A more realistic, or holistic, approach would be one that focuses on *gendered realities and gendered economic activities*. It is easy to accept the validity of criticisms directed toward agricultural programs that were established in a gender blind or gender oblivious fashion. However, one also must challenge research and programs that centre solely on one sex – as if somehow there were no relationship with the other sex and the culture in which both sexes have been socialized and now function. In short, gendered divisions of labour must be fully explored, and programs must be gender sensitive.

Taking issue with structural adjustment programs that focus on the reallocation of resources to 'economic sectors for their most efficient use', critics also contend that this male economic point of view fails to account for housework, childcare and so on. These opponents argue that what economists define as 'efficiency' actually may entail a shifting of tangible and intangible costs to the unpaid sectors (Geisler, 1993, p. 1973). There is a wealth of material on the flaws inherent in taking a purely economic, market perspective on development. These include increasing the gap between the rich and the poor, elimination of many indigenous crops, a loss of cultural diversity and biodiversity, the widening of gender inequality, and the increasing control of foreign banks, multinational corporations, and government over farmers' lives and welfare (Vander Mey, 1995). And in each case, it appears that women farmers have suffered the most.

Most funding agencies now recognize women's pivotal role in farming, so that attention has turned to what can be done about such issues. This chapter suggests that an orientation to farm family labour systems, sensitive to gendered realities and gendered economic activities, is a viable avenue for fully understanding women's needs and engaging them as participants in agricultural projects. Tapping into women's knowledge and tailoring programs to fit their needs and life schedules also are being promoted. In addition, recognizing the social and environmental importance of improved technologies for table (that is, 'women's') crops is imperative. The Clemson/Ghana IPM on Cowpea Project (a collaborative project of Clemson University, Savanna Agricultural Research Institute and the Crops Research Institute, Ghana, needs to be considered in this context. After a brief discussion of the interface between IPM and sustainable development, plus background information on Ghana, an overview of this project is given, preliminary findings are discussed, and the strategy and potential outcomes of this gender sensitive IPM project are presented. Special attention is paid to the needs of Ghanaian women farmers, gendered farming tasks and gendered realities.

IPM and sustainable agricultural development

The 'Green Revolution' was devastating to most developing nations. More people are now hungry, marginalized and homeless than before the revolution. Environments have been further degraded. Traditional diets are on the decline all over the developing world. Domestic food security has been jeopardized if not rendered severely disabled (Durosomo, 1993; Grove and Edwards, 1993; Altieri and Farrell, 1995). However, traditional farming practices by themselves are not adequate in providing basic domestic food security, let alone a full-fledged market for export. Traditional farming systems are 'outmoded and unable to meet the demands of rapid population growth, high rates of urbanization, increased mobility, and rising incomes' (Okigboo, 1990, p. 333).

Integrated pest management is a practical approach to reducing reliance on agricultural chemicals while at the same time improving the overall health of farming systems and humans. IPM has sustainability as a major theme. In reducing reliance on agrochemicals, farmers are saved the high cost of inputs – a fact that cannot be underscored enough in developing countries. Worldwide, IPM is being advocated as economically and environmentally sound. However, even though the environmental and health benefits of IPM have been recognized all over the world for some time now, in Africa the greatest push for IPM has been on the 'major,' i.e., export and cash, crops such as maize and rice (Kiss and Meerman, 1991; Altieri and Farrell, 1995; Gardner, 1996).

IPM awareness has increased in Ghana due to a series of conferences in West Africa, the successful rice IPM pilot conducted by FAO in Ghana, and governmental promotion of IPM as national policy. For Ghana and other developing countries to realize economic, social and environmental sustainability, IPM must become a regular part of *all* farming systems. Simply put, sustainable development at the macro level requires sustainability at the smallest levels. Problems of environmental degradation are linked to those of illiteracy, hunger, malnutrition and gender inequality. Participation of all – including smallholder subsistence and female farmers – is paramount for a sustainable Ghana.

Sustainable development includes initially planning small-scale, flexible projects, relying on farmers' knowledge bases, emphasizing what they are doing right and adding knowledge and insight as appropriate, providing education and training, keeping subsidies and inappropriate technologies to a minimum, and searching for solutions that ultimately can be applied in the hundreds of thousands. Including farmers in projects and working from farmers' indigenous knowledge are effective, reasonable approaches to improving the quantity and quality of agricultural products. A top-down, unilateral transfer of knowledge from the 'experts' (researchers, extension workers) will merely maintain the severe socioeconomic and socio-environmental problems crippling so many developing countries and development projects. Furthermore, more 'local' orientations may prove more socially, economically and environmentally feasible than have macro-level, science- and economics-led development schemas – especially for women farmers. Though no 'magic bullet,' participatory IPM is central to sustainability (Altieri, 1989; Bentley, 1989; Rajasekaran, Warren and Babu, 1991; Brindley, 1991; Ogunleye, 1993; Grove and Edwards, 1993; Salifu, 1993).

Ghana, West Africa

Ghana, West Africa, is considered the 'star' of Africa. Ghana was the first African nation to break from colonial rule, and the first nation in the world to implement a national development plan – in the 1920s. When Ghana became independent in 1957 it was expected to become the most developed and most democratic of all underdeveloped nations. However, by the mid-1980s a number of factors had coalesced such that Ghana seemed unable to realize its star potential. These included: political turmoil, economic stagnation, a heavy reliance on imported foods for home consumption while at the same time emphasizing the production of foods for export, deforestation and other pressing environmental problems, a late entry into a viable if painful structural adjustment program, a disproportionate emphasis on economic versus human resource development, perpetuation and exacerbation of rural–urban, farm–nonfarm inequalities and inequities, as well as breakdowns or inadequacies in the country's infrastructure (Okonjo, 1986; Chhibber and Leechor, 1993; Killick, 1995).

In the mid-1980s Ghana made economic stabilization a priority. The GDP has grown slowly but steadily since 1983, at a rate of about 3% a year. Free trade zones have been established. Multiparty democracy was restored in 1991. Participatory development is promoted. Further, the government has focused on increasing literacy and has made strides in legal and social improvements to the status of and quality of life for women and girls. (WIN News, 1992, 1996; Kamara and Denkabe, 1993; President J. J. Rawlings, 1995). Though it would be premature to declare Ghana a 'success story' in resolving its problems, Ghana is facing up to issues including poverty, hunger and malnutrition; environmental degradation; and women and girls' quality of life.[2] Participatory development is an effective approach to these problems. Growing healthier foods, and growing foods that can be used at one's own table or sold in the market, are critically important avenues of amelioration. Increasing literacy is also imperative for improving the overall quality of life for all Ghanaians – especially for women and rural residents.

Ghanaian farmers: women's special needs

Farm households are least prevalent in the urbanized coastal regions of Ghana; in the Northern and Upper West regions 90% of households are estimated to be agricultural. Most (80%) are subsistence farmers, holding an average of two to five acres (Republic of Ghana Statistical Service, 1989; World Bank, 1992).

While this is extremely relevant to the design and implementation of any farm programme, including IPM, it is very difficult to neatly summarize the issues and facts related to the quality of life of women because Ghana is undergoing rapid social, technological and demographic changes. Moreover, it is 'a rich and complex quilt comprised of many groups, religions, customs and norms, and complexities and seeming contradictions between traditional and contemporary ways and laws are interwoven and enacted in everyday life' (Vander Mey et al., 1996: 9). Women are legally equal to men, but in many areas traditional laws and norms take precedence. For instance, it is sometimes unclear whether women can own or have access to land, have the right to inherit or the right to succeed property to their daughters, or, if they are second or third wives, whether they have any rights at all! While the government of Ghana has created a series of laws and commissions to focus on the status of women and matters that differentially affect, devalue and disadvantage Ghanaian women, gaps remain between what is provided by law and what actually occurs in the lives of Ghanaian women.

Literacy, infant, child, and maternal mortality rates can be used as indicators of women's quality of life. In Ghana, about 70% of men and 50% of women are literate. Women's literacy is higher in urban areas than in rural areas, and lowest in the Northern and Upper West regions of the country. Current estimates of infant mortality range from 83 to 73 deaths per 1,000 live births, in comparison to the 1988 estimate of 85 deaths per 1,000 live births. Child mortality is currently estimated at 76 per 1,000 children. About 40% of Ghanaian mothers experience the death of at least one child. While statistics on maternal death rates in Ghana were not obtainable, available reports state that the rate is 'high enough to be a social problem' and that maternal death is most prevalent in the rural, and especially the rural Northern, regions of the country (Republic of Ghana Statistical Service, 1989; WIN News, 1992; World Bank, 1992; Macro International, Inc., 1995).

Benneh (1994: 10) states that in Ghana 'the unequal distribution of labour among men, women and children is normally not an issue raised in development policies since it may be generally assumed that men and women jointly and equally share the responsibility of family maintenance'. Benneh contends however that just as it is inappropriate to use Western models of the nuclear family when studying family life in Ghana, it is equally inappropriate to maintain the Ghanaian orientation in which the man is the sole provider.

The Clemson/Ghana IPM on cowpea project

As noted by Asafo-Adjei and associates (1995), cowpea is 'the second most important grain legume in Ghana in terms of production and consumption'. The legume is an important source of protein whether consumed after drying or fresh; leaves and pods also have protein value. Most farmers with whom we have interacted, declare cowpea important for consumption and for cash. Its value as a foodstuff is recognized as

Training of trainers in Tamale, Ghana

greatest during the lean season. Women farmers tended to inform us that cowpea are becoming even more important now that people are discovering more interesting ways to cook it. In addition, they in particular have told us that cowpea are absolutely necessary in the diets of babies and pregnant women. Finally, research clearly documents that Ghanaian women farmers have played a significant role in the preservation of cowpea seed and genetic sources (Bennett-Lartey and Akromah, 1996).

The Clemson/Ghana IPM on Cowpea Project[3] is a multidisciplinary effort to implement IPM for this important crop. Ethnographic surveys have been conducted, cultivars from South Carolina and Ghana have been tested for pest resistance, early blooming cowpeas have been developed and IPM pilots have begun in farmers' fields. Using the successful Indonesian model (Wiradmadya and Kusmayadi, 1996), Training of Trainers (TOT) was inaugurated in the Northern Region of Ghana – the major cowpea-growing region of the country – in July 1996. After TOT, Farmer Field School training will begin. As described in later chapters, in these Field Schools researchers, plant protection personnel, extension workers and farmers all learn together. They cover crop growth habits and requirements, preparing healthy soil to produce a healthy crop, signs of disease and pest infestation, basic IPM practices such as scouting, and the difference between pest and beneficial insects.

Planning and implementation are guided by the following assumptions:
- farmers' indigenous knowledge is vital to IPM;
- projects are successful when farmers are partner participants;
- women's vital roles – and typical inequality – in the farm family and the farming economy must be fully considered;
- women farmers' knowledge, needs and practices should inform any farm project;

- extension agents' attitudes towards and service delivery to women farmers must be taken into account in all stages of research and project implementation.

That is, to be successful, both planning and implementation must be gendered. The team is cognizant of criticism of previous development and agricultural schemas. The project thus explicitly requires the inclusion of women farmers, extension workers and researchers. All farmers, male and female, are *participants* and, as opposed to earlier studies that focused on the 'woman question' by looking at the internal household, interviews and surveys attempt to tap the entire farm family economic system – including contributions made by children.

When this chapter was written, the project was in its initial phases. The aim of the project is to increase yields, promote additional production of cowpea as a valuable protein source, improve the environmental health of farms, decrease health hazards associated with agrochemical use, increase profits and empower subsistence and women farmers.

Gendered farming activities

Interviews with Ghanaian farmers (n=20) and pilot IPM implementors (n=17) demonstrate that more research on farm family labour systems is needed and that IPM implementation must recognize the existing diversity among family systems. The gendered division of labour historically associated with Ghana is that men clear the land and women do the planting, harvesting and carrying to market. Our interviews show that tilling tends to be done by men or men and boys, but is sometimes hired out, as is land clearance. Planting and harvesting are now more often shared among family members, rather than assigned by sex and age. However, marketing is still primarily a 'woman's activity', one which is very time-consuming and usually results in little monetary reward for women.

Getting water is still primarily a female or child activity. This too can be very time consuming. One farmer reported that women or children went for water two or three times a day. Each trip took about 30 to 45 minutes. Another farmer said that on her farm, children get water about three or four times daily. Depending upon the season and hence the availability of water, trips take between 20 minutes and three hours. Gathering firewood and tending cooking fires are other extremely time-consuming tasks typically relegated to women and children. Child care, housecleaning and cooking – which can take as much as seven hours per day – are still basically seen as girls' and women's tasks. Boys are usually assigned animal tending duties, while mending clothing is seen as an individual responsibility that one may hire out to women seamstresses (Vander Mey, 1995; Vander Mey et al., 1996).

Gendered realities

While gender issues in agriculture are beginning to be addressed, I suspect an invisibility of women as farmers lingers in some regions of Ghana. For instance, one field agent laughed at the concept of 'women farmers'. Apparently, in his view, men farm and the women just 'help out'. I suggested to him that women who farm no doubt define themselves as farmers; in point of fact, all women interviewed did give their occupation as 'farmer'. I suspect this agent may not be alone in his thinking, and it is vital to be aware of this potential barrier.[4]

Furthermore, while the division of labour is changing in some regions, women farmers still have heavier, more continuous workloads than men. There also is a real leisure gap between farm men and farm women. In addition, farm women disproportionately suffer the effects of poverty and inequality – including illiteracy, poor health, barriers to bank credit, and tenuous access to land (Vander Mey et al., 1996).

Other findings

Interviews showed that farmers use cowpea as a cash crop, a weaning food, a traditional food and as animal feed. Given better prices and more recipes, cowpea is increasingly popular. Farmers recognize cowpea's significance in the diets of pregnant and nursing women, in babies' diets and in getting through the lean season. While few farmers can regularly afford agrochemicals, those who do use pesticides typically fail to protect their bodies, use agrochemicals indiscriminately and engage in haphazard if not dangerous methods of pesticide storage and container disposal. If this can be done without a decline in yields, some farmers would be willing to reduce agrochemical use for health and economic reasons. Interviews also documented the relatively heavy workloads of women farmers, thus signalling that IPM on cowpea must not add to their loads.

Pilot IPM

Using neem in pilots on farmers' fields was initiated in August, 1995 as the first action component[5] of the project implemented. Neem's efficacy in farmer field conditions has been tested in each growing season since. Neem is readily available, and results indicate that neem-based IPM is cost and time efficient. Yields from neem-treated cowpea were competitive with those from the agrochemical-treated and control fields. Using neem as a natural pest control appears efficacious for men and women farmers alike. Farmers participating in the pilots were 'untrained.' They focused upon applying neem at certain stages of growth in response to particular indicators of pest infestation. Subsequent interviews indicated a need to make distinctions between beneficial and pest insects: one farmer, for instance, said that bees are insects that must be killed.

Three other major action components have since been introduced: Training of Trainers, farmer field schools, and the cowpea action research sites. As noted, Training of Trainers was inaugurated in the Northern Region in 1996. Thirty-four Ministry of Food and Agriculture (MoFA) staff[6] participated. In 1997 and 1998, 35 and 32 MoFA staff members respectively were trained in this participatory in-field, nonformal approach to learning how to apply IPM to cowpea. TOT participants learn about cowpea varieties and their resistant qualities, growth habits, stages at which insect pests and beneficials are most likely to appear, scouting, signs of pest and disease infestation, pest-beneficial complexes, safe handling and storage of chemicals, bodily protection when using chemicals, and effective storage techniques. Trainers then are empowered to help organize and conduct Farmer Field Schools. FFS content is similar to what is learned initially by trainers, with the addition of farmers' indigenous knowledge and practices. FFS began in 1997 in the Upper West Region with 25 farmers. In 1998, 30 farmers were trained in the Northern Region. Both TOT

Woman farmer with backpack sprayer (northern Ghana)

and FFS are based on the four IPM principles still being successfully used in Indonesia and elsewhere in South and Southeast Asia: grow a healthy crop, observe fields regularly, conserve beneficial organisms, and develop human resources. In the process, the farmer becomes the expert.

Finally, a cowpea action research site (CARS) was inaugurated in Ejura in 1998. CARS is a multidisciplinary, multi-institutional, farmer participatory approach. It emphasizes cowpea production in a farming systems context, and the 'process' rather than testing finished products. The approach is based on the Indonesian model of the action research facility. It provides an opportunity to unify efforts toward the common goals of increasing the production and consumption of cowpea in West Africa. What is added here includes researchers, more technical, scientific aspects of cowpea varietal selection, and IPM (Vander Mey, ed., 1998).

Gender sensitive IPM: strategy and potential outcomes

This cowpea project has been gender sensitive since its inception. Ethnographic studies were conducted to glean the gendered and cultural realities of Ghanaian farmers. Both the US and Ghanaian research teams included women. The TOT included women extension and plant protection personnel. This is especially important because women researchers and extension workers can facilitate the participation of women farmers who otherwise would not be included or, due to traditional norms and a lack of recognition of women as farmers, otherwise would not participate. Furthermore, by tapping into women farmers' indigenous knowledge, this project should broaden and strengthen the database regarding the significant roles Ghanaian women play in the preservation of seed and genetic sources (Bennett-Lartey and Akromah, 1996). It is assumed that as men farmers see and learn from women farmers, women will be recognized as farmers. Women should emerge as farm 'experts'. Women as well as men will be encouraged to become 'master farmers'. They will train other farmers and enlarge the circle of farmers participating in sustainable development directed toward better health and a better environment. Farmer field schools should further develop the participatory aspects of the programme.

Outcomes thus far[8]

At the end of a TOT/FFS session the increase in self-confidence among the participants is noticeable. Participants 'know' more and feel more confident about growing healthy cowpea, others know the signs of pest infestations and so on. Participants quickly grasp the basic tenet that good IPM starts with growing a healthy crop. As one TOT participant said, 'Before this school what we taught frontline staff and farmers about pest control in cowpeas was simply that they should spray on calendar dates and/or indiscriminately any time they see an insect species settled on the crop. Now it will be different. Not all insects are harmful to the crop. We need to preserve natural enemies.'[9]

A focus group evaluation of the FFS conducted in the Northern Region in 1998 showed farmers agreed to attend the FFS to gain knowledge and new skills, and to obtain higher cowpea yields. Prior to the field school, none of the farmers could identify insect pests of cowpea. At evaluation, all participants could identify five pests. Several also mentioned that they now know how to minimize pesticide use, and are more informed about the potential hazards of chemical use/ misuse. Finally, several participants mentioned that they had picked up valuable communication and teamwork skills, which they now can use in other settings.[10] The multiplier effect we are seeing from the FFS is very telling here. When asked, 1998 FFS participants said that at a minimum, each was teaching at least ten other individuals. Married men in this group indicated that this included their wives.

Perhaps the most important outcome of FFS thus far is that identified by a woman farmer: 'Cowpea production need not be by using insecticides all of the time. These chemicals are dangerous and even expensive. In this training programme we have learned that inspecting your crop allows you to find out if there are enough beneficial insects to take care of the pests and also that we can use other products such as neem extracts to control the pests on cowpea.'[11] In a focus group interview held with CARS participants at Ejura during their second session, about fifteen women farmers actively participated. They stated unanimously that one of their primary reasons for giving up valuable time to the CARS was that they needed and wanted the knowledge it would provide. Women also said they were attending the CARS so they could teach their husbands and other family members, make a profit, and improve their farming; this would make it possible to provide for their families more adequately.[12]

Challenges

A great challenge to this project is the need to very sensitively tailor IPM to reduce pest and weed problems on women's crops, while not increasing women's labour.

Ideally, in the long run IPM should reduce the time women spend in the fields. It might even reduce the need for outside labour. If this should occur, it will prove to be a real bonus to women farmers, who tend to have fewer money reserves than men farmers.

Another challenge is the gendered leisure gap, which some may say has no relevance to this project. All the same, men have more leisure time than women. It is possible that the Farmer Field Schools will not only facilitate a sharing of knowledge and expertise between men and women, but also may serve as a catalyst for more sharing of farm tasks. That, indeed, could speak to a sometimes intangible, yet very real, improvement in the quality of life for women farmers and their families.

Another challenge is locating and timing FFS and TOT to accommodate the heavy workloads, for women in particular. Thus, for instance, off-season FFS may be necessary, if women are less pressed by other duties at that time. An off-season TOT has met with success, so an off-season FFS might as well. We also recognize that among some groups, wives who do not attend the sessions will be taught by their husbands afterwards. If that is the arrangement, then the facilitators must make every effort to encourage this transfer of knowledge, and also must applaud the men who follow through.

This is a small and slimly funded project. However, combined with other participatory agricultural projects, it should help to facilitate the Ghanaian quest for sustainable, participatory development.

Notes

1 Associate Professor, Department of Sociology, Clemson University, Box 341513, Clemson, SC, USA 29634-1513.
2 For statistics and policies pertaining to these problems, please contact the author to request a copy of the 1996 report (Vander Mey et al.) listed in the references.
3 USAID grant no. DAN-1310-G-SS-6008-00. Principal Co-Investigators Dr. B. M. Shepard and Dr. B. J. Vander Mey of Clemson University, Dr. A. B. Salifu of Savanna Agricultural Research Institute, Tamale, Ghana, and Dr. M. Owusu-Akyaw of the Crops Research Institute, Kumasi, Ghana.
4 At the same time, it is important to emphasize that this was the response of only one extension agent. Overall, the Clemson/Ghana project has enjoyed a rich collaborative relationship with the extension service in Ghana. The team is currently conducting a national survey of extension agents to find out exactly what their perspectives are with regard to the nature and needs of Ghanaian farmers.
5 Additional, more technical aspects of the project include surveying cowpea fields to determine major pest and beneficial species (predators and parasites); identifying and evaluating pest resistant varieties; and determining crop losses and action levels required to contain pest outbreaks. The current paper, however, focuses on implementation of IPM with farmers.
6 Including their Women in Agricultural Development specialists.
7 Vander Mey wrote and edited this publication based on contributions from the entire Clemson/Ghana team. B. M. Shepard provided the discussion of CARS.
8 We have developed an instrument to allow us to quantitatively and qualitatively evaluate the impact of these various schools. Baseline information has been taken and post-project follow up will commence soon. Ideally, we will wait a few growing seasons before the follow up in hopes of getting a clearer picture of retention of knowledge and extent of training being provided others, as well as other retrospective evaluations that will suggest ways to improve these schools.

9 FY 96 Annual Report of the project.
10 Conducted by Vander Mey, with B. M. Shepard and A. B. Salifu.
11 Co-Principal Investigator Dr. A. B. Salifu, Savanna Agricultural Research Institute, Tamale, Ghana provided this quotation. It also appears in the FY 97 Annual Report on this project.
12 Conducted by Vander Mey.

Bibliography

Altieri, M.A., 'The question of small farm development: who teaches whom?' *Agriculture, Ecosystems and Environment*, vol. 9 (1989), pp. 401–405.

Altieri, M.A. and J.G. Farrell, *Agroecology: the science of sustainable agriculture*. Boulder, CO, Westview Press, 1995, pp. 433.

Asafo-Adjei, B., K.O. Marfo, G. Atuahene-Amankkwa, M.A. Hossian, M. Owusu-Akyaw, and J.V.K. Afun. 'Cowpea breeding research in Ghana: past, present and future'. Crops Research Institute, Kumasi, Ghana, 1995. (Poster presentation at 2nd World Cowpea Research Conference, Accra, Ghana, West Africa.)

Barrett, H. and A. Browne, 'Environmental and economic sustainability: women's horticultural production in the Gambia'. *Geography*, vol., 76 (1991) pp. 241–248.

Beckley, S., 'The burden of development'. *Connexions*, vol. 41 (1993) pp. 10–11, 32.

Benneh, G., 'Family and development in Ghana: an overview'. In: E. Aradayfro-Schandorf, (ed.), *The family and development in Ghana*. Accra, Ghana Universities Press, 1994.

Bennett-Lartey, S. O. and R. Akromah 'The role of women in plant genetic resources activities in Ghana'. *Plant Genetic Resources Newsletter*, vol. 106 (1996), p. 43.

Bentley, J.W., 'What farmers don't know can't help them: the strengths and weaknesses of indigenous technical knowledge in Honduras'. *Agriculture and Human Values*, vol. 6 (1989) no. 3, pp. 25–31.

Blumberg, R.L. 'Toward a feminist theory of development'. In: R.A. Wallace (ed.) *Feminism and sociological theory*. Newbury Park, CA, Sage, 1989, pp. 161–199.

Brindley, B., 'What is 'sustainable?' *Ceres*, vol. 128 (1991), pp. 35–38.

Chalfin, B. 'Adjusting society: The World Bank, the IMF and Ghana'. Book review in: *Africa Today*, vol. 44 (1997), no. 4, pp. 465–468.

Chhibber, A. and C. Leechor, 'Ghana: 2000 and beyond'. *Finance and Development*, September 1993, pp. 24–27.

Durosomo, B., 'Technology adoption and sub-Sahara African agriculture: the sustainable development option'. *Agriculture and Human Values*, vol. 46 (1993), pp. 99–121.

Gardner, G. 'Preserving agricultural resources'. In: L.R. Brown (ed.), *State of the World 1996*. New York, W.W. Norton 1996, pp. 78–94.

Geisler, G., 'Silences speak louder than claims: gender, household, and agricultural development in Southern Africa'. *World Development*, vol. 21 (1993), pp. 1965–1980.

Grove, T.L. and C.A. Edwards, 'Do we need a new development paradigm?' *Agriculture, Ecosystems and Environment*, vol. 46 (1993), pp. 135–145.

Kamara, S. and A. Denkabe, *A handbook on participatory approach to training: project planning management and animation*. Accra, Freedom Press, 1993.

Killick, T., 'Structural adjustment and poverty alleviation: an interpretive survey'. *Development and Change*, vol. 26 (1995), no. 2, pp. 305–331.

Kiss, A. and F. Meerman, *Integrated Pest Management and African agriculture*. Washington, DC, The World Bank, 1991.

Kraus, J., 'The struggle over structural adjustment in Ghana'. *Africa Today*, vol. 38 (1991), no. 4, pp. 19–37.

Macro International, Inc. 1995. *Nutrition of infants and young children in Ghana: a decade of research findings from the Demographic and Health Surveys program.* (Produced by Africa Regional DHS Nutrition and Family Analytical Initiative Project.) Calverton, MD, Macro International, Inc., 1995 (NetScape).

Ogunleye, B., Chief. 'Local initiative: key to women's voices in global decision making for a healthy environment in Africa'. *Women and Environments*, vol. 13 (1993) nos. 3, 4, pp. 15–16.

Okigboo, B.N. 'Sustainable agricultural systems in tropical Africa'. In: C.A. Edwards, R. Lal, P. Madden, R. H. Miller and G. House, *Sustainable Agricultural Systems.* Delray Beach, St. Lucie Press, 1990, pp. 323–352.

Okonjo, C. 'The concept of development'. In: C.K. Brown (ed.), *Rural Development in Ghana.* Accra, Ghana Universities Press, 1986, pp. 3–25.

Rajassekaran, B., D.M. Warren and S.C. Babu, 'Indigenous natural resource management systems for sustainable agriculture development: a global perspective'. *Journal of International Development,* vol. 3 (1991), pp. 387–401.

Rawlings, J.J. President of Ghana. Address by H. E. Flt. J. J. Rawlings. World Summit on Social Development. Copenhagen, Denmark. (Electronic version prepared by the World Summit for Social Development by the United Nations Department of Public Information. March 11, 1995, NetScape).Republic of Ghana Statistical Service, 1989.

Salifu, A.B. 'Integrated Pest Management'. Paper presented at the Association of Church Development Projects, Navrongo, Ghana, 1993.

Vander Mey, B.J. 'Gendered planning and implementation of a cowpea IPM programme in Ghana'. Paper presented at the International Plant Protection Congress, The Hague, The Netherlands. July 1995. Social Science Reports 9604-2. Clemson, SC, Clemson University, Department of Sociology, 1995.

Vander Mey, B.J. (ed.), 'Integrated Pest Management on cowpea in Ghana: accomplishments and future aims'. Paper prepared for and distributed at the Bean/Cowpea CRSP, PEDUNE, RENACO, IITA/ILRI Cowpea Review and Planning Meeting, Ibadan, Nigeria. March 1998.

Vander Mey, B.J., A.S. Langyintuo, W. Mulkey, J.S. Brown and J.E. Hawdon, 'Using farmer information to enhance farmer field school training: the case of IPM on cowpea in Ghana, West Africa'. Social Science Research Reports 9607-2. Clemson, SC, Clemson University, Department of Sociology, 1996.

WIN News. 'The status of women in Ghana: from the report of Ghana to the committee on the elimination of discrimination against women'. *Women's International Network News*, vol. 18 (1992), no. 2 (Summer), pp. 50–51.

WIN News, 'Ghana: the national council on Women and Development'. *Women's International Network News*, vol. 22 (1996), no. 4 (Winter), p. 60.

Wiradmadya, R. and A. Kusmayadi, 'Indonesia: National IPM Programme'. Programme Advisory Committee Meeting. FAO Intercountry Programme for IPM in Asia. Hyderabad, India, February 1996.

World Bank, World Development Report. New York, Oxford University Press, 1992.

Lisa Bradshaw[1]

5 Women's roles in crop protection decision making: the case of Atenas County, Costa Rica

This study was conducted in Atenas County, Costa Rica, located approximately 40 km northwest of the capital city, San José. The area is characterized by the cultivation of coffee, citrus and mango fruits and basic grains; over 70% of farms produce some combination of these crops. There is also some cattle ranching. Settlement of the region occurred relatively long ago in Costa Rican history and over the generations the tradition of sub-parcelling land has led to the prevalence of 'minifundios', or plots of land too small for subsistence. Given the proximity of San José (one hour by bus) and another urban centre approximately 20 km away, many individuals, particularly male heads of households, commute daily to jobs in the city. Although the repeated divisions of farms and ease of daily commuting are conditions fairly specific to Atenas, I will argue that Costa Rican government policies including structural adjustment as well as laws promoting women's rights are having similar effects on women's responsibilities on family farms across the country. In short, as the possibility for a family to derive economic survival from farming diminishes, men increasingly seek off-farm employment, leaving women to shoulder greater responsibility for semi-subsistence production.

During my work as an agroecologist, primarily in crop fields, I observed that women were rarely visible at any stage of IPM projects. This research project began in December, 1994 as a result of my own personal curiosity and desire to work more closely with women. With the cooperation of a colleague and several willing students,[2] farm women (148 women from a population of approximately 20,000 people) were interviewed about their roles, sources of crop protection information, and types of learning workshops that would interest them. This chapter is based on the results of these interviews and my interpretation of probable dynamics of women's roles in farming, given the current sociopolitical climate in Costa Rica. With these results and the conclusions they suggest, opportunities for enhancing women's participation and empowerment in crop protection become evident.

Women's roles on small farms

Rural women's involvement in agricultural labour is widely recognized, although official figures have often underestimated their participation. Campillo and Fauné (1993) cite a 1993 study by the Inter-American Institute for Cooperation on Agriculture/Inter-American Development Bank (IICA/IDB) which reports that women represent 8% and 12% of the economically active population (EAP) in Costa Rica and Latin America plus the Caribbean, respectively. Counting individuals who perform non-domestic activities as part of the EAP, however, increases these percentages to 24–28% and 20–35%. Furthermore, the same study found that 70–80% of rural women spend up to four hours per day on agricultural tasks. These tasks typically include specific chores, among them preparing plant nurseries, weeding, harvesting, raising small animals and performing post harvest processing and storage. Other studies, such as Malena (1994) on Africa and on Indonesia (see Chapter 8), also report these same activities (not necessarily exclusively) as generally being in women's labour domain. In Central America women provide 54% of the labour to maintain home gardens, with children providing another 16.3% (Radulovich, 1994).

The results of our study in Atenas County reflect similar trends. Many times when women were initially asked about their farms or gardens they would reply that they didn't have any, until the interviewer inquired specifically about the crop plants and animals visibly roaming about the property. Perhaps these women tended to consider their crops and livestock of lesser merit than their own abstractions of a full farm, since they now serve to supplement the family diet more than to generate cash income. Once the presence of crops and/or livestock was established, 73% of women interviewed named some farm activity they perform and 40% specifically stated that they tend their home gardens. When asked who made the decisions regarding pest management on their family's farm however, the majority of women referred to a male head of household – husband, father, brother or son (see Table 1).

Table 1 'Who makes pest management decisions on your farm?'[a]

Response	Per cent
Male household head	56.5
Female household head	2.7
Male and female share decision	10.9
No answer	29.9

[a] 148 women interviewees

Why are women not involved in pest management decision making?

To try to determine what factors contribute to women's lack of decision power in the area of crop protection, we ran a number of correlations. The results follow.

- Women's participation in pest management decisions was not related to their age, amount of education (two-thirds had not studied beyond primary school), participation in community groups or the source of crop protection information they reported.

- However, women who received this information either with or instead of male household heads were more likely to make these decisions.

These results are hardly surprising; most likely they simply provide a specific example of a widespread situation. In fact, the literature examining the exclusion of women from development projects in general, and more specifically those dealing with agricultural technology transfer and extension, amply illustrates this point (see Vander Mey, Chapter 4, for a review).

The obvious follow-up question, 'What prevents women from gaining access to pest management information?' has been examined in both general (e.g. Gabriel, 1990) and more specific senses (e.g. van de Fliert, Chapter 7). Broadly stated, constraints include time conflicts with domestic chore loads; cultural perceptions of agriculture as 'men's' work, leading to underrepresentation of women in training, extension and so forth; lack of confidence among individual women to participate in male dominated activities; and men not liking or refusing permission for their wives to participate in courses, workshops or conversations with other men.

To address this question specifically in Atenas County, we asked women about their sources of pest management information and which family member(s) receive it. Table 2 shows the responses given, broken down by gender of recipient. Interviews were then conducted with the most widely cited sources of information, the Ministry of Agriculture (MAG) extension office and a local agricultural cooperative (Coopeatenas), to learn about their extension activities and how women fit into them. Coopeatenas offers biannual bulletins including farming information, holds on-farm demonstrations, and gives four regular seminars timed to fit the stages of coffee production as well as other seminars in response to specific community requests related to other crops or pest problems; a full time extension agent is employed. Information and invitations to seminars are sent out to registered members. Their list is made up of individual names, although the extension agent sees 'members' more as family units than as individuals. Currently, women comprise approximately 20% of the more than 1200 names on the membership roster; thus many women must at least know when and where seminars occur. However, in our surveys only 2.8% of those asked (108 individuals) said they had attended one. Seminars are held in the late afternoon, which for women may present a time conflict with preparing dinner. When asked what he saw as the reason for the apparent low participation of women in the seminars, the extension agent replied that he thought women simply were not interested in the topics.

Table 2 'Where do you receive information on crop protection?' by 'Who receives the information?'[a]

Source	Female head/both	Male head
Coopeatenas	14	34
MAG extension office	11	22
Neighbours/friends	11	24
Agricultural supply store salesperson	6	20
Own ideas	4	11
Other (e.g. books, magazines)	4	6

[a]148 women were interviewed, although 26 did not answer these questions; also, several women named more than one information source. Thus percentages do not necessarily add up to 100. For 'recipient of information,' women were allowed only one choice

Technical assistance from the Atenas MAG extension office includes on-farm demonstrations and visits as well as seminars requested by farmers, in which anyone can participate. Other collaborative projects that involve working with groups of producers are also underway with organizations such as the United Nation's Food and Agriculture Organization (FAO). Interestingly, the agent in this office is female, which theoretically should lower some barriers to women who wish to participate. She noted, however, that female attendance in seminars was very low.

Women interviewees were given a list of topics ranging from cake decorating to pest management to 'any other option' and asked to select themes on which they would be interested in attending workshops. There was no limit on the number they could choose. More than 30% of the women selected pest management and/or home garden management as one of their choices. This indicates that low female participation in agricultural seminars is not simply a matter of lack of interest. Furthermore, the third most widely cited source of crop protection information for women recipients was neighbours and friends, indicating that this is sometimes a concern and topic of conversation among them.

The fact that women are interested in learning about crop protection is arguably reason enough to make efforts to include them. Additionally, as individuals involved in food production, women should share in decisions regarding any aspect of productive activities, and thus they need enough knowledge to take informed decisions. In the current social order in Costa Rica, women are generally the primary caretakers of children; as such, they will give their offspring the values and context in which they will view human actions in farming and the larger natural world. Table 3 shows women's perceptions about the use of agrochemicals on their family's farm, illustrating that many women would like to see fewer chemicals used, but in the majority of cases they said that decreased use is contingent upon alternative pest control options. If we accept IPM as part of a broader movement toward sustainable development, then training women in ecologically based pest control may insure that specific methods and, potentially, a broader environmental ethic emphasizing natural species interactions, will be embraced by the next generation. Beyond these reasons though, it can be argued that women's roles on small farms are increasing as a result of social and political policies, and therefore their capacitation in crop protection merits particular attention.

Table 3 'What do you think about agrochemical use on your farm?'[a]

Response	Per cent
Amount used is necessary and adequate	27.7
Should increase amount used	1.4
Should decrease amount used[b]	47.3
Don't use any	2.0
Don't know	4.7
No answer	16.9

[a]148 women interviewees
[b]26.4% specified that use should be decreased if other options are available

Structural adjustment and women's changing roles

Policy programs commonly known as structural adjustment have been imposed on developing countries around the globe in recent years. The focus of structural adjustment is on debt repayment through:
- decreases in government spending, generally achieved by lowering public employment and decreasing spending on social programs;
- promotion of industrialization by opening up to foreign investment;
- attempts to increase export earnings by promoting agricultural exports.

The implementation of structural adjustment has had various consequences for rural areas. Urban migration has increased as men and women seek jobs in industry. In Latin America for example, rural poverty increased in the period 1980–1989 (Trejos, 1992). In Costa Rica, emphasis on export crops such as bananas, cattle and a variety of 'non-traditionals' has decreased the credit available to producers of internally consumed food crops. With the exception of rice and sorghum producers, these are disproportionately small farmers (Chiriboga et al., 1992). Furthermore, production of export crops necessitates a means of transporting produce from the farm to the exterior. This is only efficient on a relatively large scale, particularly since perishable items often require refrigerated containers. These conditions put small farmers at a disadvantage in attempting to produce non-traditionals like flowers, fruits and mini-vegetables, thus exacerbating their deteriorating economic situation. As a consequence, small farm families increasingly need salaries from off-farm employment to meet basic needs. The male head is often the first family member to seek outside work; women stay on the farm taking on the added responsibilities created by their husband's absences. IICA (1991) provides several case studies and analyses of rural Latin American women's workloads, showing the increases that have resulted from recent economic policies.

In Costa Rica, progressive social policy changes may also be increasing women's responsibility on farms. Among other provisions, the 'ley de promoción de igualdad social de la mujer' (law for promotion of women's social equality) passed in 1990 changes registration of property to allow for title to be held by the family instead of an individual (who was usually the man) as well as providing women equal access to agricultural credit. While from 1962 to 1988 women accounted for only 11.8% of the individuals given land titles by the 'Instituto de Desarrollo Agrario' (Institute for Agricultural Development, the government office responsible for land reform), they received 38.7% of the titles issued in 1990 (Chiriboga et al., 1992). Also, in cases where marital or other unions are terminated, the 'Codigo de familia de Costa Rica', (1973) (Costa Rican family code) generally favours the woman retaining the house, and presumably part of the surrounding land that was previously family property.

In summary, recent social and political policies are leading to increases in the presence and responsibility of women on small farms in Costa Rica. In Atenas County cultural patterns that over many generations have resulted in smaller and smaller parcels of land have had similar results. This offers another, final reason to specifically include or target women in the generation and transfer of crop protection technologies.

Opportunities to increase women's knowledge and participation

The level of interest among the women surveyed in workshops on pest and/or garden management, plus their opinions on agrochemical use on their farms, clearly demonstrate the potential for greater female participation in crop protection. Our experiences in workshops held around the County in different neighbourhoods reinforce this perception. Although a few men did attend in one instance, we targeted women by specifically inviting them to workshops on composting household wastes and making insect repellents from plant extracts. Techniques for composting and multi-uses (as repellants and/or for medicinal use) of plant species were shared with interest. Broader discussions on the impact of conventional, i.e. high input, agriculture on human nutrition and health also arose among those in attendance. At one workshop in particular the women present expressed an active interest in meeting again to exchange information on various related topics and suggested that coming together in the garden of one participant might be an even more effective setting for learning.

We specifically extended invitations to these workshops only to women, because for our purposes it was important to determine the potential for their attendance. However, this strategy is unlikely to be adopted by Coopeatenas or the MAG extension office. Given scarce resources and cultural biases, they may logically feel that holding separate seminars/ training for women would be redundant or an inefficient use of human resources. Nevertheless, within the broad theme of agricultural production they could encourage additional women to participate through their choice of training topics. For example, to date neither Coopeatenas nor MAG has offered any seminars on home garden management or other areas that typically make up women's work. In Atenas, addressing such topics in seminars could be an appropriate way to adjust to current farming trends, first because more women might be inclined to participate; and second because as land parcelling continues, more and more farms are being perceived as or transformed into large home gardens.

Conclusion

This study has examined women's roles in farming in Atenas County, Costa Rica, but many of the conditions and results are not unique to this location. Although women are generally involved in farming activities, they are often excluded from access to crop protection information, thus precluding their ability to participate in decisions on these issues. Nonetheless, changing socioeconomic conditions and policies as well as cultural patterns are positioning women as small farm managers, who have more intimate or frequent contact with the land than their mates. This increase in responsibility, along with other reasons elaborated in the text, including equity, need for knowledge-based decisions, the mother's role in passing on values and the potential impact of women as a stimulus to a new environmental ethic, calls us to scrutinize gender roles in traditional pest management extension and define possible opportunities to promote women's empowerment, as crop protection managers as well as environmental stewards.

Notes

1 School for Field Studies, Centro de Estudios sobre Desarrollo Sostenible, Dept SJO 2122, Box 025216, Miami, FL 33102, USA.
2 Collaborators on this continuing project include fellow faculty José Luis Diaz and the following alumni: Deborah Simon-Weisberg, Noreen Slevin, Tina Fiasconaro, Megan Dymzarov, Ned Bourne, Alexis Kerner, Amy Sidran, Gillian Weber and Josh Wood. Views presented in this paper are the author's own and should not be interpreted as necessarily completely shared by other collaborators.

Bibliography

Campillo, F. and M.A. Fauné, *Gender, women and development: a framework for IICA's action in Latin America and the Caribbean*. San José, Instituto Interamericano de Cooperación para la Agricultura, 1993.

Chiriboga, M., R. Grynspan and L. Pérez E., *Mujeres de maíz*. San José, Instituto Interamericano de Cooperación para la Agricultura, 1992.

Gabriel, T., 1990. 'Pest management, women and rural extension'. *Tropical Pest Management*, vol. 36, no. 2 (1990), pp. 173-176.

IICA, (Instituto Interamericano de Cooperación para la Agricultura), *Mujer y modernización agropecuaria: balance, perspectivas y estrategias*. San José, Instituto Interamericano de Cooperación para la Agricultura, 1991.

Malena, C., *Gender issues in integrated pest management in African agriculture*. Chatham, UK, Natural Resources Institute, 1994.

Radulovich, R. (ed.), *Tecnologiasproductivas para sistemas agrosilvopecuarios de ladera con sequia estacional*. Turrialba, Costa Rica, Centro Agronómico Tropical de Investigación y Enseñanza, 1994.

Trejos, R. (ed.), *Ajusto Macroeconómico y Pobreza Rural en America Latina*. San José, Instituto Interamericano de Cooperación para la Agricultura, 1992.

Catrin J. Meir[1]

6 Improving women's participation in pest management training: a pilot study in Honduras[2]

What little pest management training is available to rural people in Honduras is almost entirely directed at male farmers. Yet smallholder families in Honduras tend to function as a unit; if we want to enable rural families to change and improve their pest management, we need to offer training to all members of that unit – men, women and children. There are also ethical issues at stake: women have as much right to learn as men, and it is important that training programmes actively strive to provide equal access to information, quite apart from the confidence building and empowerment that occur during effective training. Finally, some of the best pest management strategies have been invented by farmers – both women and men. If we exclude half the rural population from the opportunity to learn more about pest management, we may well lose some very valuable ideas, not to mention important allies in the fight against the indiscriminate use of pesticides. Training for women should therefore be seen as a necessity, as well as a right.

This chapter looks first at the involvement of women in agriculture in Honduras and why women have largely been ignored in the provision of training in general, and pest management training in particular. It also considers why women are often unable to attend training on the rare occasions when it is offered to them. The Natural Pest Control training offered to smallholder farmers by the Pan-American School of Agriculture is then summarized. A pilot study conducted by the Hillsides IPM Programme with two groups of women in two different villages in Honduras is described, together with its impact six months further on. The final section presents conclusions and recommendations for making pest management training more available and more useful to rural women.

Women, agriculture and training in Honduras

Women's role in smallholder agriculture

At first glance it is easy to assume that Honduran women do not need pest management training. In Honduran society, the dichotomy between the roles of men and women is strong. Men generally hold the purse strings, have most of the decision making power and all of the mobility. Women, on the other hand, are entirely responsible for childcare and other domestic work, and are often effectively tied to the home. All of this makes women much less 'visible' to the outsider – and since, unlike most men, they are often busy from dawn until dusk, they also tend to have little time to explain the extent of their responsibilities to outsiders or to answer probing questions. Nonetheless, women play an important role in agricultural production. At the very least they are responsible for food storage and preparation, washing clothes contaminated with pesticides and caring for family members who may have intoxicated themselves with pesticides. Women are also involved in purchasing inputs, and some (especially those from indigenous groups) work in the fields alongside the men. A small but increasing number of women, often encouraged and supported by local NGOs, are starting home vegetable gardens where they are responsible for all aspects of crop production. In addition to these various roles, many women must take overall responsibility for the family's crop production, either while their husbands are ill or away doing seasonal work, or perhaps full time, having been abandoned by the father of their children.

Why is women's participation in training so low?

Despite the fact that women are an integral part of the smallholder production system, men tend to be the focus for outside interest because they tend to have a higher profile in the community. Thus invitations to training courses, especially in the realm of agriculture where the women's role is often less obvious, generally go almost exclusively to men. However, this is not the only reason for the low number of women attending training courses. Many training courses require their trainees to be literate. Even those organizations which do not *demand* literacy explain that the farmers who attend training are usually those who can read or write, since pre-literate farmers tend to feel inadequate and ill at ease in training sessions. As the literacy rate among rural women is even lower than that of men, this effectively excludes a great many women. A third problem is that even if a woman is invited to attend training and feels sufficiently literate and confident to go, she may well be unable to do so unless she has an older daughter or a female relation or neighbour who can look after her children and feed her husband for her while she is gone. This is a particularly important issue where training sessions last a whole day, or worse, several days, and take place in training centres rather than in the community. Finally, even if all the above difficulties can be overcome, there are also cases where the woman's husband is unwilling for her to attend training, and without his permission she cannot go.

As a result, only a tiny minority of women receive any form of pest management training. Those who do attend training are often the more literate, better-off women with fewer family ties, and perhaps some link with the local extension agent. Since women who are elected by outsiders do not necessarily make the best 'change agents', this can result in the development of 'information pockets' that remain locked up within those members of the community who are already the most advantaged, leaving the majority without any opportunity of benefiting – thus further exacerbating existing social differences.

Zamorano's Natural Pest Control training

The Pan-American School of Agriculture, based in Honduras and better known as Zamorano, offers pest management training to men and women smallholder farmers from all over Central America. The training, which is run by the Hillsides IPM Programme of the Department of Crop Protection, grew out of the work of anthropologist Jeffery Bentley, and is based on the principle of respecting and complementing farmers' knowledge through interactive, participative training. The aim is to share ideas with farmers, rather than transfer 'recipes'; the overall goal is to stimulate farmers to adopt and invent pest management strategies that do not depend on pesticides. The trainee farmers have dubbed the training 'natural pest control', reflecting the fact that the course highlights the many different ways farmers can try to manage their pest problems by manipulating the natural environment. All aspects of pesticide use, other than their effect on natural enemies, are excluded in an effort to redress the existing national and regional imbalance, since most of what little pest management training is available concentrates exclusively on pesticides.

The farmers and farmer-extensionists who attend the training courses are chosen by local NGOs, through which the training is arranged. The courses last two to three days and are held locally or in Zamorano's training centre, depending on logistics. The training is equally suitable for literate and non-literate farmers, and the only cost to the farmers is their own time for attending. Zamorano currently offers two training courses; one in insect management, developed by Jeffery Bentley, Gonzalo Rodríguez and Ana González, which began in 1991 (Bentley et al., 1994), and one on plant disease management, developed by Steve Sherwood with Myriam Paredes (Sherwood, 1995 and Paredes Chauca, 1995), which began in 1994.

Even though Natural Pest Control training is offered to both men and women farmers, only 10% of the approximately 6,000 farmers trained by 1995 were women. However, those women who have attended have been very interested in reducing the use of pesticides, and many have made significant contributions to this goal. Doña Theodora, for example, is a part time extensionist for a small NGO and a vigorous champion of non-chemical pest management. Doña Blanca, who works with a different NGO, attends training with her husband whenever she can – indeed, in his place, when he is

Doña Hubalda, inventor of one of the most popular pest management strategies to come out of Zamorano's natural pest control course: spraying sugar water to attract natural enemies

unable to go – and is the driving force behind the family's pest management choices. And Doña Hubalda, a link farmer for the Honduran government, is the inventor of possibly the most successful pest management technology developed by a farmer as a result of Zamorano's natural pest control course: spraying sugar water to attract wasps and ants, which then eat caterpillars and other pests (see Cañas Cañas, 1996 for an evaluation of this technique). Experience with the Disease Management Course indicates that not only can women come up with original pest management strategies with broad appeal for smallholder farmers, but also that their presence in groups of trainee farmers seems to stimulate more inventiveness among participants than occurs in groups consisting of men alone (Sherwood, 1995).

In view of the very positive experience gained to date in training women, we decided to conduct a pilot study aimed at encouraging as many women as possible in the communities selected to attend. The objective of the study was to gain a better understanding of factors that affect attendance at and subsequent use of pest management training for women. For the sake of simplicity, we decided to concentrate on the insect management course.

Training for women only: a pilot study

Sites and participants

We decided to hold training courses in two very different communities, one Ladino (i.e. people of mixed Indian and Spanish blood) and one of indigenous Lencans,[3] both of whom had expressed interest in pest management training. The women of the Ladino community, Sendero Quebrado, were typical in that most of them did not work in the fields, but tended to stay close to the house preparing food, looking after children and tending largely ornamental home gardens of varying sizes. Although Sendero Quebrado boasted a community building, the women were not organized into a group. The Lencan women of Tres Cruces, on the other hand, worked in the fields alongside their husbands whenever their domestic and child care duties allowed this. Besides taking an active part in their own crop production, they were organised into a group that farmed about two hectares of land communally.

A comparison of the agriculture of the two communities is given in Table 1. Insecticides were the main form of pest control in both communities; their use was regular, with a large proportion of calendar, prophylactic spraying, but had not reached the two-to three-day frequency common in some areas of Honduras. In both communities the purchase of insecticides necessitated a trip to the nearest town: this took 1–2 hours each way and the cost of the return trip was roughly equivalent to one day's wage for each community.

The training we offered was restricted to women only, to encourage as many women as possible to attend and to overcome any possible deference to men that might result within a mixed group. We had not found this a problem previously, since the few women who had been able to attend our courses had been fairly self-confident and outspoken. However, the experience of a colleague in trying to include larger numbers of women was that most women tended to keep quiet in mixed groups, at least in the beginning. 'In a discussion they wait until the men have spoken and then they agree with what the men have said. So we try and train women and men separately, at least until the women have gained enough confidence to participate fully in a mixed group.' (Judith Castro, personal communication.)

The courses were held in the community in each case, so that as many women as possible could attend. The training was given in February/March, just before the growing season started, and covered two half days. The only reason for the women to attend was their own interest: no external incentive was offered. The women themselves set the times for the training and brought their own food where the course lasted over lunchtime. We were careful to specify that the training involved no reading or writing requirements, and that mothers with small children could bring them along.

Table 1   Comparison of cropping systems in study communities

	Sendero Quebrado	Tres Cruces
Altitude	800m above sea level	1600 m above sea level
Cropping seasons	Two three-month growing seasons in the May–November rainy season	One nine-month growing season for maize; consecutive three-month seasons for potatoes
Crops	Maize, beans and some vegetables; surplus sold	Potatoes a cash crop; maize and beans for home consumption; surplus maize sold
Main insect pests	In maize	In maize
	- grass loopers	- fall armyworm
	(*Mocis latipes*, Lepidoptera)	(*Spodoptera frugiperda*, Lepidoptera)
	- fall armyworm	- white grubs (*Phyllophaga* sp., Coleoptera)
	(*Spodoptera frugiperda*, Lepidoptera)	In beans
		- *Diabrotica* and other Chrysomelidae leaf beetles (Coleoptera)
	In beans	In potatoes
	- *Diabrotica* leaf beetles (Coleoptera)	- white grubs (*Phyllophaga* sp., Coleoptera)
	- weevils (*Apion godmani*, Coleoptera)	- potato weevils (*Phthorimaea operculella* and/or
	- leaf hoppers	*Scrobipalposis solanivora*, Coleoptera)
	(*Empoasca* sp., Homoptera)	- wire worms (Elateridae, Coleoptera)
	In ornamentals and others	In vegetables
	- leaf-cutter ants	- various caterpillars (Lepidoptera)
	(*Atta* sp. and others, Hymenoptera)	- harlequin bugs (*Murgantia histrionica*, Hemiptera)

All-women training sessions: laughter and learning

The training sessions in both communities covered three main themes: insect reproduction, insect predation and the manipulation of natural enemies (i.e., the effect of pesticides on natural enemies, and how to encourage the presence of more natural enemies on the farmers' land). As always with the Natural Pest Control training, the emphasis was on sharing new ideas and building these new ideas into the trainees' existing knowledge. This was achieved by drawing out the knowledge the trainees had, using questions to elicit information little by little. In this way, trainers helped trainees to realize how much they knew and to build bridges from an old idea, such as knowledge of bee reproduction, to a new idea, such as caterpillar reproduc-

A popular exercise early in training: women using what they have learned to separate insects caught in their own fields into 'helpful' and 'harmful' (without allowing insects to escape from the plastic bags). Mirth as well as awe and wonder resulted: 'So many friends were out there helping us when all we were doing was killing them, because we didn't know'

tion. The development of these ideas was stimulated by using slides and real insects, including predatory insects eating their prey, all of which helped trainees take a closer look at what goes on in their fields. The training was participatory and dynamic, making use of energizers,[1] discussions and practicals as well as question and answer sessions. Each course also included several brainstorming sessions in which participants developed potential pest management strategies for the most important local pests, using the new information they had discovered.

The training sessions were shorter than the usual three-day training course offered by the Hillsides IPM Programme, so we were not able to spend as much time on each new concept as we normally would (between two and three hours per concept, instead of four to five hours). There was therefore less repetition of the new ideas than in our standard courses. There was also an important difference between the two communities: in Tres Cruces we were able to put into practice some of the pest management strategies the women suggested in group practicals. This was not possible in Sendero Quebrado because there was no communal plot available.

Both groups of women loved the training, its practical nature and the way they were encouraged to participate and were treated as equals by the trainers. They were interested and proud to be learning about a world they had not realized existed right under their fingertips. They told us it was particularly important for them that this training was offered to women, in their own communities, and at times they could manage, since what training did exist was nearly always held in nearby towns and almost exclusively directed at men. (Many women got up an hour or two earlier than the usual 4.30 am to get most of their domestic chores done in time to attend. Those with pre-school children brought them along.) Of the fifteen to twenty women invited in each community, eleven attended in Sendero Quebrado and fifteen in Tres Cruces, so the training sessions were slightly smaller than the usual size of about twenty to twenty-five.

None of the women had participated in any pest management training before, most of them were not literate and almost all were initially very shy, especially the Lencan women. However, in the face of the trainers' enthusiasm for sharing new ideas and their respect for and interest in the women's own knowledge, the women soon lost their reserve. There was a higher level of energy and more laughter and enthusiasm early on in the training than we generally saw with groups of men, who often took longer to relax and join in fully. Although the Lencan women knew more about pest management than the Ladino women, both groups had less knowledge at the start of the training than was usual with men. Nonetheless, the women learned quickly and seemed to embrace new ideas more readily than men. By the time the course was over, all of the women had a good grasp of the concepts presented and how some of these could be applied to their local pest problems. They were delighted with the training, enthusiastic about the possibilities of putting some of what they had learned into practice, and hoped very much that there might be some follow-up training in the future.

Impact after six months

When we returned to evaluate the impact of the training, we found quite different results in the two communities. Six months to a year later, the women of Sendero Quebrado retained the basic ideas of insect reproduction and predation, but most had forgotten essential details, such as the life cycles of key pests, or which insects were beneficial. There were one or two isolated cases of women trying out non-chemical alternatives on the largely ornamental plants around their houses, for example applying ash to control sap suckers and smearing resin around the trunks of citrus trees to deter leaf-cutter ants, but on the whole there was very little application of the knowledge gained. Some of the women of Sendero Quebrado had tried to share what they had discovered with their husbands, but most had met with resistance to what were very new concepts for the men. Women were not seen as credible sources: for example, listening to one woman explain to her husband what she thought about a pest problem, it was clear that he was did not believe that she, a woman who spent most of her time in the house, could possibly know anything about the subject – much less be right.

The situation was different in Tres Cruces. Six months after the training, more than half of the women remembered all the life cycle details of two or three key pests. A further third remembered most correctly. All of the women were able to mention two or three natural enemies; three or four women mentioned six or seven. Much more significantly, the practical impact of the training was also quite different. About two-thirds of the women had tried out one or two of the pest management practices they had come up with during the training. The most popular strategy was to kill any caterpillar or harlequin bug eggs encountered in fruit and vegetable crops: the women had previously been unaware that these eggs hatched out into pests. Some of the women had dug over their land more thoroughly to expose white grubs to predators, and several had tried making light traps to kill the adult beetles, which they had previously not connected with the grub. One woman had applied earth to the corn whorl of maize plants to kill fall armyworms and two others had tried new crop associations to reduce pest damage. As a group, the women had revived the partially abandoned practice of piling up the remains of the previous year's maize crops around their communal potato plot, where it not only acted as a barrier to reduce soil erosion, but also provided a refuge for natural enemies. They were also leaving weeding their maize field as long as possible, partly to conserve moisture and partly to avoid destroying the flowers growing up around the maize plants: the flowers were attracting wasps, which the women now recognized as useful predators.

Most women had shared some of their new ideas with someone else in their family, and one or two shared some of what they had learned with a neighbour. Acceptance of these ideas was much less than 100%, and while the men still seemed to consider it unlikely that the women might know something they did not, women appeared to have less of a credibility problem than in Sendero Quebrado. Nonetheless, new practices were most often being implemented on land the women controlled themselves rather than on family plots, which were largely controlled by men, with women contributing their labour.

Interestingly, however, a chance visit to Sendero Quebrado a year and a half after the training showed that the seeds of change were still present, though dormant. A local NGO had begun encouraging women to cultivate vegetable gardens to add vitamins and variety to their diets without having to make expensive trips to town markets and pay high prices. The NGO had made sweet pepper seeds available to the women at reduced cost and shown them how cultivate these plants. One woman we visited was having problems with her sweet peppers: they were all bad inside. Pulling one apart we asked what she saw. 'It's some kind of disease,' Doña Ana said, squashing the mess with her thumb. We showed the chilli to her eight-year-old son, who was keen to join in the discussion. Encouraged to look inside, he pushed the discoloured bits of sweet pepper around with a grubby finger. 'There's worms,' he announced, winkling out a white grub a few millimetres long. Doña Ana looked more closely and was forced to agree. From there, with a little prompting, she worked out the life cycle of the pest (the sweet pepper weevil, *Anthonomus eugenii*, Coleoptera) on the basis of what she had learned during the Natural Pest Control training course the previous year. She quickly decided that instead of leaving the bad peppers to rot, thereby encouraging the weevils to breed, she would collect them up and bury them. We explained when the adult weevils lay their eggs and told Doña Ana about the different ways other farmers had tried to reduce this problem without using pesticides (crop hygiene, crop combinations and botanical insecticides applied at flowering; see Meir, submitted.) When we left, she and her son were busy collecting the rotten chilli peppers in a large gourd, planing to bury them away from her vegetable plot.

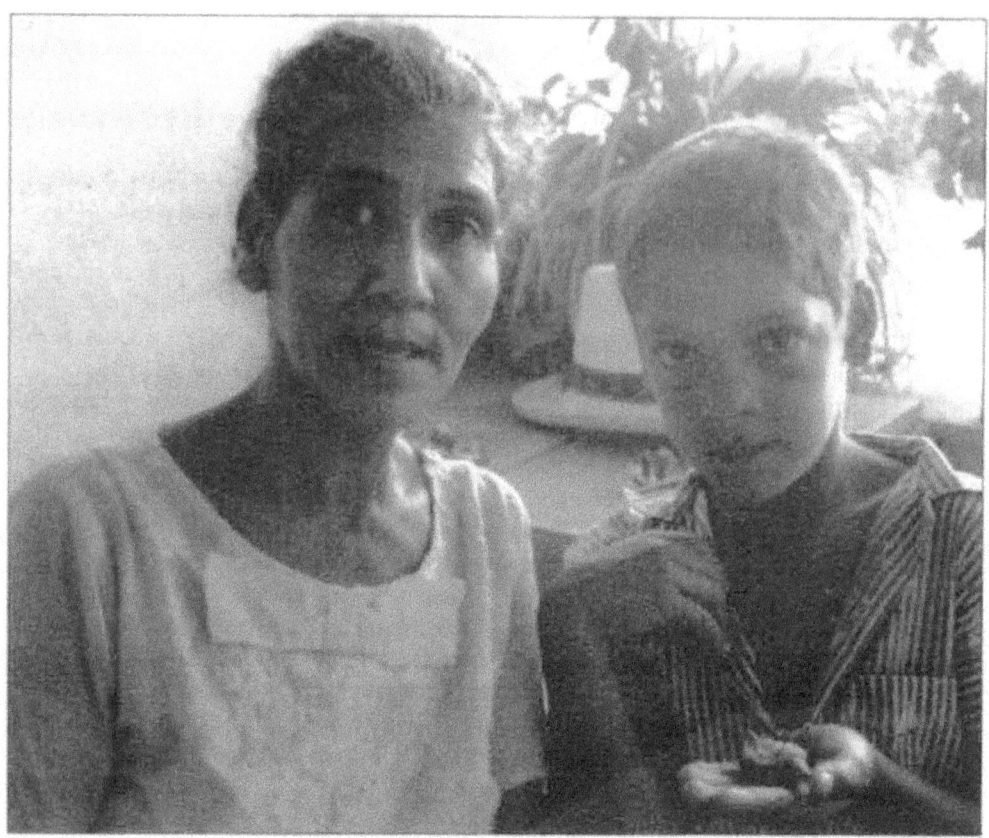

Doña Ana and her son: he discovered that weevil grubs, rather than a disease, were attacking their sweet peppers. Using what Ana had learned during training, they decided to collect and destroy all infected peppers to break the weevils' life cycle

Conclusions and recommendations

Although this was a very small scale study, we feel the difference in the impact seen in the two communities highlights a number of issues. The main constraints limiting women's attendance at training (being invited, being able to attend and potential embarrassment due to illiteracy) can be addressed by carefully arranging and structuring training. Even though their knowledge may initially be less than that of men, once they are able to attend, women can clearly enjoy and benefit from pest management training, whether they work in the fields or remain close to home. However, if training is to have maximum impact, even courses such as the one on natural pest control (which is based on general concepts rather than on specific pest management practices) will need to be adapted to local circumstances, to make it more useful as well as more accessible to women. If we can achieve both of these goals, then even the most reluctant menfolk may begin to feel that it is a good thing for their women to participate!

The following pointers for increasing the likelihood of success are based on what we have learned.

Arranging training

Ways to encourage as many women as possible to attend:
- make training available to all women in the community and check (as far in advance as possible) to be sure they all know they are invited;
- offer the training within the community, at times chosen by the women themselves;
- encourage women to bring their younger children along. Be prepared to cope with the disruptions and noise this may entail, and where possible actively involve the children in the training.

'Women only' training, at least initially, seems to encourage the participation of women who might otherwise be too shy to attend. (But remember that restricting attendance to members of any one particular group of women may exclude disadvantaged segments of the community.)

Structuring the course

Beware of trying to fit in too much in one go. We compared the results of the training described here with other, longer, courses in which there was time to cover each idea more thoroughly. We concluded that spending less time on new concepts did seem to result in less learning, and therefore probably also affected confidence in the new ideas and motivation to try them out. A total of at least four hours for each new concept (reproduction, predation etc.) may be a good working minimum. Given the typical restrictions on women's time, it would be preferable to split up training into smaller sections, permitting in-depth treatment of new ideas; and to present it over a period of weeks, rather than in two or three days. The practicalities of reaching isolated rural communities makes this a good case for training local NGO extension agents to give the training themselves.

Don't know doesn't mean can't learn

Don't be put off by an apparent lack of knowledge at the start. Even indigenous women spend less time in the field than their male counterparts, so that they may know less initially. But both field-going and home-based women can learn and apply new concepts if they are motivated and have the opportunity to put their new ideas to the test.

Meeting needs

Tie the training into the participants' own felt needs, not just into local pest problems as perceived from the outside. Ensure that participants can put their new knowledge into practice: if no such opportunity exists (e.g. their agricultural work is limited to the largely male-controlled areas of family crop production), it is important to create one. Linking pest management training for women to projects related to home gardens seems to offer good potential, particularly where some assistance with start-up inputs such as seeds is available. Actually having a nearby plot to try out some of the new pest management strategies women come up with as part of the training, as opposed to just discussing them, appears to significantly increase the use of these practices after the training.

Training the family unit

Ensure that both men and women have access to training. The women's apparent lack of credibility with their husbands and the scant information passed on to wives by men who participate in training (Meir, submitted) seem to make clear that if we are to help rural families work together to reduce their pesticide use and make better use of the resources that surround them, we need to train all members of the family unit. Training women and men separately appears to be a more useful approach (at least initially), given that this allows us to adapt both the content and logistics of courses to suit individual participants. Training should also be provided for children, since they can play an important role, whether with their mothers in home gardens or with their fathers in the fields. Children may act as a stimulus, both by encouraging their parents to try new practices and as keen observers and repositories of ideas and details their parents may initially forget. And, of course, they are tomorrow's farmers!

Women and pest management: future potential

We hope that by using what we have learned and working in collaboration with local NGOs we will be able to train many more women in the future. We want to continue to learn from the women who participate in our training as well as to share new ideas with them, so that as we gain experience we will be able to keep adjusting our training to meet women's needs more closely. We feel that more women trained in Natural Pest Control, with more experience of and confidence in 'alternative' pest management strategies, will lead to a reduction in the indiscriminate use of pesticides. Women are often the members of the community who have the most to gain from improvements in their families' health and the local environment. Through their own actions, and through interaction with their husbands and children, they have the capacity to make important contributions to changing the tide of pest management towards a more sustainable future through greater use of local resources.

Notes

1. The names of the communities in this study have been changed to protect the anonymity of the women who took part.
2. I am very grateful to the British Economic and Social Research Council, which funded this study through the Imperial College Centre of Environmental Technology of the University of London, and to Zamorano, the Pan-American School of Agriculture in Honduras, which supported the fieldwork. I would like to thank all the members of Zamorano's Hillsides IPM Programme for their help and support, and in particular trainers Myriam Paredes and Antonio Oseguera, who were a joy to work with and who put so much effort into making the training a real learning experience for all involved. Thanks are also due to Kathy Colverson, Cesar Cardona and Judith Castro for help in the field, to Jules Pretty, Steve Sherwood, Stephanie Williamson and John Mumford for helpful comments on earlier versions of this paper and, of course, to the women of Sendero Quebrado and Tres Cruces.
3. Honduras has a population of approximately five million people, about 90% of whom are Ladino. The remaining 10% is made up of various indigenous groups who live mainly in the highlands, the lowland rainforests or along the coast. The Lencans are one such group, living in the highlands in the west of Honduras.

4 Energizers (also known as group dynamics exercises or, in Spanish, *dinámicas*) are games used to raise energy levels during training, and are very popular in Latin America. (For some ideas on energizers see Vargas Vargas, 1992, Vargas Vargas, 1993, and Pretty et al., 1995.)

Bibliography

Bentley, J.W., G. Rodríguez and A. González, 'Science and people: Honduran campesinos and natural pest control inventions'. *Agriculture and Human Values*, vol. 11 (1994), pp. 178–183.

Cañas Cañas, L.A., 'A response of natural enemies to sugar applications in maize and their effect on fall armyworm *Spodoptera frugiperda* (J.E. Smith) populations in Honduras'. Purdue, Purdue University, 1996. (MSc thesis.)

Meir, C., 'Training for change: evaluation of participatory training in natural pest control for smallholder farmers in Central America'. London, University of London, Imperial College Centre for Environmental Technology. (PhD thesis, submitted but not vivaed, November, 1998.)

Paredes Chauca, M.C., 'Evaluación del impacto de la capacitación en enfermedades de plantas para pequeños agricultores en tres comunidades de Honduras'. Honduras, Escuela Agrícola Panamericana, 1995. (Ingeniero Agronomo thesis.)

Pretty, J., I. Guijt, J. Thompson and I. Scoones, *Participatory learning and action*. London, International Institute for Environment and Development, 1995.

Sherwood, S., 'Mastering mystery: learning to manage plant disease with farmers of Honduras and Nicaragua'. Cornell, University of Cornell, Ithaca, USA, 1995. (MPS thesis, agriculture.)

Vargas Vargas, L., *Técnicas participativas para la educación popular. Tomo I*. Costa Rica, Centro de Estudios y Publicaciones Alforja, 1992.

Vargas Vargas, L., *Técnicas participativas para la educación popular. Tomo II*. Costa Rica, Centro de Estudios y Publicaciones Alforja, 1993.

Elske van de Fliert[1]

7 Women in IPM training and implementation in Indonesia

The importance of women's role in agriculture has been widely acknowledged (e.g. Boserup, 1984; Sajogyo, 1983; IRRI, 1985; Shiva, 1989; Siwi et al., 1990), but has seldom received specific attention in agricultural development programmes. In most cases this lack of attention has meant that males automatically become the target group for community programmes. In Indonesia this is usually a result of a general assumption that heads of families will be men, who are also expected to represent their households in formal village activities. That is, while the exclusion of women from training programmes does not seem to have been intentional, as will be seen below, it has nevertheless had observable effects that require correction.

In crop cultivation the distribution of tasks between women and men seems to depend mainly on the type of crop and on local cultural habits. For instance, rice cultivation in several areas of Central Java involves women in transplanting, weeding, routine observation of the crop, supplying food for hired labourers, harvesting and threshing, drying and selling the harvest; men are responsible for preparing the soil, preparing and caring for the seedbed, supervising transplanting, managing water and fertilizer, making routine observations of the crop, controlling pests, and harvesting and selling the harvest or supervising these activities (van de Fliert, 1993). In vegetable cultivation in North Sumatra, however, we see women involved in all crop cultivation tasks, including preparing the soil and spraying pesticides. It is obvious that women have a very important role in decision making in all cases, since women usually manage the household's money.

Before looking at women's role in integrated pest management (IPM), we should first differentiate various categories of women farmers. In Indonesia, three main groups of women farmers can be distinguished:
• women who manage their farm together with the husband;
• women whose husbands are temporary migrants. Usually this means the husband leaves the village to work in the city after the crop has been established, returning just before harvesting (although some return at the fertilization stage and others only for the establishment of the next crop);
• women who manage the farm on their own, because they have no husband or the husband is permanently away.

Surveys indicate that 17% of Indonesian agricultural households are headed by women in the third category, managing on their own (FAO, 1990). The responsibility for farm management decisions is especially great for these women farmers, as well as those in the second category. Particularly for these women, involvement in agricultural development programmes would be extremely useful. However, they often belong to the lower socioeconomic layers of the community (van de Fliert, 1993) who in general are overlooked by development programmes (Röling, 1988) – which implies that these women are doubly neglected.

Women's role in agricultural decision making and activities clearly indicates a need for their active involvement in IPM training and implementation. Obtaining a critical mass of women who are knowledgeable about IPM will significantly increase the effectiveness of its spread throughout farming communities. This chapter will first describe how women's tasks in agriculture are related to IPM, and how they have so far been involved in IPM programmes in Indonesia. An analysis is then made of the constraints and opportunities for actively involving women in IPM training and implementation.

Women farmers and IPM

IPM, as presently advocated in Indonesia, is a crop protection approach that emphasizes the specific ecological and economic conditions of individual farms, as well as farmers' ability to take informed crop protection decisions based on routine observations of the crop and its environment, plus analysis of farm conditions (Pincus, 1991). For various crops and various areas of Indonesia, it has been shown that farmers implementing IPM principles are able to reduce their expenditures on farm inputs while often producing higher yields than non-IPM farmers, so they increase their profits. Practices important for IPM implementation include choosing suitable, pest resistant varieties; good field preparation; adequate field sanitation; production of healthy seedlings; appropriate water and fertilizer management; timely and adequate weeding and pest control measures; and timely harvesting. The key to success with IPM seems to lie in the adequacy and timeliness of all management practices, producing a healthy crop and a healthy ecosystem that can resist pest and disease attack. To take adequate and timely decisions, farmers need to carry out routine monitoring and analysis of the crop ecosystem.

IPM is a complex, knowledge-intensive approach; it has many aspects that need to be known before a farmer can take informed decisions in accord with IPM principles. For example, types of pests and diseases and ways to assess the damage they can cause to a crop, types of natural enemies and their role in the crop ecosystem, analysis of comparative costs of different types of pest control, and effects of pesticides (and other control measures) on human and environmental health are all important aspects of the knowledge needed. This complexity means that training is required.

Many of the IPM practices mentioned above relate to farming responsibilities held by women. The importance of the decision making process, including the potential for savings on farm inputs, also call for their involvement in IPM implementation. In addition, women's exposure to pesticides often entails even greater risks, since through them pesticide residues can affect other family members. This is true not only because of their reproductive roles but also their other tasks: women are usually the ones who prepare the food for the family and serve as the caretakers. Therefore, it is especially important for women to be well informed about the hazards of pesticides and the ways to reduce their use. Yet as is amply demonstrated in this book, training provided for men alone does not 'trickle across' to women. For all of these reasons, it is vital to involve women in training.

Involvement in IPM training

In Indonesia, IPM training for farmers and field staff is presently the responsibility of two major programmes: the National IPM Programme and the World Education

IEMA programme, although increasing numbers of NGOs are adopting the model. The National IPM Programme, launched in 1989, is managed by the Indonesian government in collaboration with the UN's Food and Agriculture Organisation (FAO). The 'IPM Farmer Field School' model presently being applied in a variety of Asian countries was developed by the FAO technical assistance team within the Indonesian National IPM Programme. This model includes field-based, season-long training and emphasizes discovery and learning by experience. World Education (WE), a US non-governmental organization (NGO), initiated the IEMA ('Improved Environmental Management and Advocacy') programme in Indonesia in 1991. This programme also emphasizes IPM development and training, but works through a network of local NGOs and farmer groups. The Farmer Field School model of the National Programme is used here too, but is adjusted in several ways to fit the needs and conditions of NGO communities. Additionally, the WE programme has experimented with the field school model as an arena for participatory technology development in crops such as cabbage, potato, hot pepper, soybean and groundnut, where as yet there are no sound IPM technologies.

Figure 1 Women's participation in Indonesian National IPM Programme FFS: first training cycle[a] versus 1995/1996[b]

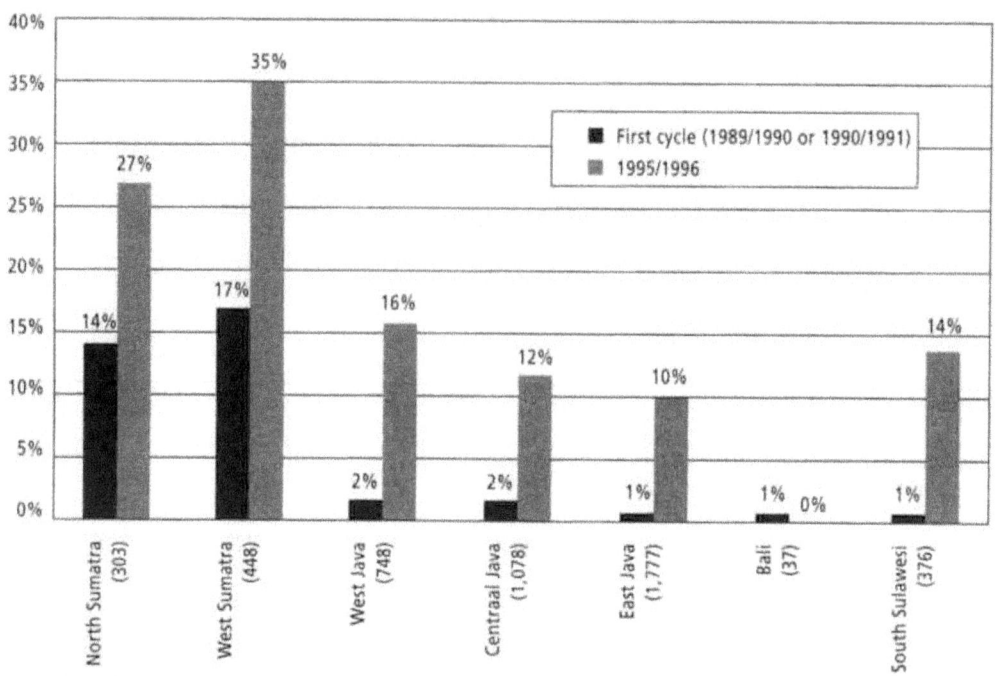

[a] The first cycle was in 1989/1990 or 1990/1991, depending on the province
[b] Women's participation is shown as a percentage of total number of participants; numbers in parentheses indicate the number of Farmer Field Schools implemented per province during the 1995/1996 training season

Sources: van de Fliert, 1993; Kingsley and Siwi, 1996

Women's participation in National IPM Programme IPM Farmer Field Schools has been measured in several studies (Figure 1). During the first training season (1989/1990 in North Sumatra, Java and South Sulawesi, and 1990/1991 in West Sumatra and Bali), a total of 1,700 FFS were organized; women appear to have been involved in only 19% of these groups, and in 15% of groups there were five or fewer women participants. On average, only 3% were women – just one person among the twenty-five participants per group.

When these data are analysed by province, great variation of women's involvement in IPM Field Schools is visible. North Sumatra (where most of the agricultural workload is borne by women) and West Sumatra (which has a matrilineal culture) show a relatively high number of women participants, 14% and 17% respectively. These percentages, however, are still low compared to the proportion of farm work done by women in these areas, which is more than 50%. In all other provinces women are equally involved in rice farming compared to men (except for Bali where women are more confined to the house to fulfil religious ceremonial functions), yet the number of women attending IPM training was extremely low in the first training cycle (2% or fewer).

While these data show some influence of cultural differences on the involvement of women, in general women were indirectly screened out: trainees were selected from the members of the organized farmer groups, which are usually made up of the men in the communities. Moreover, the selection of trainees was left to the village extension workers, who were not given explicit selection criteria; they in turn often handed this responsibility over to village officials. In this situation it is reasonable to expect that habitual patterns will be followed, resulting in the selection of men, who are seen as heads of the households, to participate in training. Even the men who are chosen may not be the most appropriate. This was observed in a study in Central Java, where all Field School participants were not only men, but primarily men from the higher and middle socioeconomic layers in the village (van de Fliert, 1993). The wives of these men were often not directly involved in farming; either they had off-farm employment, or their families were prosperous enough to hire farm labour. Therefore, many of these wives were not informed by their husbands about what they had learned in the Field School. Further, such men usually have little or no communication with women in lower socioeconomic layers. As a result, in these villages there was no dissemination of IPM messages to women farmers, who mostly belong to the lower socioeconomic layers.

In the first years of World Education's IPM training activities in Central Java and North Sumatra women's participation was never analysed quantitatively, but it is estimated that the proportion of women participants was below 10%.

Neither the National IPM Programme nor the World Education Programme ever purposely intended to exclude women farmers from their activities. However, a lack of deliberate attention to their involvement – as in most development programmes – means that women are often indirectly excluded. As one village extension worker said when he was asked why his training groups did not contain any women, 'Well, I never thought about it!'. Deliberate and specific action is needed to break through cultural habits (which are not necessarily barriers) to actively involve women in agricultural training and development activities.

After realizing this, both the National IPM Programme and the WE Programme have successfully begun taking steps to increase women's participation in programme activities. WE has developed a training preparation process, during which a gender analysis using various tools and a needs identification are carried out together with the farming communities and village officials. This process makes possible a more just participant selection for IPM Farmer Field Schools. The idea of the preparation process has been adopted by the National IPM Programme and adapted to the conditions of government extension mechanisms. The results are obvious: women's participation in IPM Farmer Field Schools has increased substantially over time (Figure 1). In general, village officials and men and women farmers also respond positively to deliberate requests to actively involve more women. However, by 1995/1996, the National IPM Programme target of 25% women participants had been attained only in the provinces of North and West Sumatra; nevertheless, deliberate action has produced a good start on enhancing women's access to learning about IPM.

Women's role in IPM Farmer Field Schools

Interviews with Field School graduates (both women and men) from some mixed composition groups in North and West Sumatra and Central Java showed that the presence of women in training groups had a positive effect on the training process. With the exception of presentations of ecosystem analyses and experiments, which were left mostly to the men, women participated actively in all activities. Only women trainees with relatively high education dared to stand in front of the group and give a presentation. In small group exercises, women's performance was equal to that of men. Many men stated that the women in their group were more accurate in observing pests and natural enemies; this forced them to take a better look.

All women participants interviewed stated they had enjoyed the Field School and that this experience had been very valuable for their daily work on the farm. After the Field School, they felt more able to take decisions on crop management in general and pest control in particular. This helped them to economize by avoiding unnecessary expenses for farm inputs.

Using cartoons is one way to make training materials attractive and increase their impact. The ways women are depicted can encourage trainees to see women as people who can be involved, competent FFS participants

First picture suggests the woman is an equal and interested candidate in the process of participant selection. In the second, a woman is shown playing an important role in the crop production decision making process

Increasing involvement: constraints and opportunities

As stated above, in the implementation of the Indonesian IPM programmes cultural habits initially hampered the involvement of women in IPM training, although these habits do not necessarily seem to form an impenetrable barrier. On the other hand, despite the encouraging finding that as a result of a better participant selection process the number of women participants has increased in recent years, some constraints that seem more difficult to resolve can be detected. First, women farmers are usually also housewives, with the additional tasks of taking care of the household and the children. They have hardly any leisure time. Also, because household tasks are often difficult to schedule, it is harder for women than for men to guarantee that they will follow the Farmer Field School process routinely over an entire season (that is, attending weekly sessions). Second, Indonesian women often feel less competent than and inferior to men, which can hamper their active involvement in training. Even though it is generally the woman who manages the household and decides household matters, in the outside world she is supposed to act submissively. A third set of constraints in some areas, such as the North Sumatra highlands, are local customs: husbands there do not like (and sometimes even do not allow) their wives to be involved in an activity with other men and/or with a male facilitator.

To reduce or even nullify such constraints, each situation will need to be analysed separately. Both opportunities and barriers presented by local customs and cultural habits will need to be explored together with the local community. For instance, to what extent can men be asked to take responsibility for particular household tasks while their wives attend training? To what extent can Field Schools be scheduled so they will not interfere with the duties of women farmers/housewives? To what extent and in what ways can women be stimulated, convinced and empowered, to obtain more self-confidence? Is it feasible to set up special women's training groups and/or to find women facilitators? And, probably the most important aspect: can a selection procedure that enables and encourages the involvement of women farmers in IPM training be designed and implemented?

Here it should be noted that one solution often suggested as a way to increase women's involvement in training – often applied but unlikely to yield any sustainable result – is the appointment of women participants who are relatively well educated (Sumayao, 1986). These women often show a high level of interest and an ability to play a prominent role in Field Schools, but their involvement in day to day farming is often negligible. In several cases it has been observed that more educated women Field School graduates leave the village after the training season is over to look for work, particularly office work, in the city. Relatively high education should not be a selection criterion for IPM training; what counts is daily farming experience and high motivation to implement and develop what is learned in the Field School.

A gender study recently done for the National IPM Programme summed up ways to further enhance women's access to and role in IPM training in Indonesia (Kingsley and Siwi, 1996) by recommending the following actions:
- broad application of the preparation process prior to conducting an IPM Field School, including a gender analysis;
- strengthening the role and training of farmer trainers and extension workers in this preparation process, and ensuring adequate and timely funds for application of such a

process; and
- strengthening women's leadership development.

Only when such processes have been institutionalized in the existing extension mechanisms can women's involvement be assured in the long term.

Conclusion

The desirability of involving women farmers in IPM implementation makes it imperative to assure their recruitment into IPM training. Thus far, however, the number of women participating in IPM Field Schools in Indonesia has been relatively low, due to lack of attention to gender issues in IPM programmes. Special efforts are therefore needed to increase women's involvement. Programmes should make deliberate efforts to design selection procedures and training schedules that enable and encourage the active participation of women farmers, in particular those belonging to the lower socioeconomic layers in the community, who most need information and training that will allow them to improve their decision making capacity and hence their farming practices. This will mean actively working with farming communities prior to conducting a Farmer Field School, to carry out a preparatory process of gender analysis. This makes it possible for communities and trainers to analyse and resolve constraints, including cultural habits and customs, that hamper women's active involvement in training and development activities.

Note

1 IPM Specialist, International Potato Center (CIP ESEAP), Bogor, Indonesia.

Bibliography

Boserup, E. Peranan wanita dalam perkembangan ekonomi. Jakarta, Yayasan Obor Indonesia, 1984.
Fliert, van de E., 'Integrated Pest Management: farmer field schools generate sustainable practices. A case study in Central Java evaluating IPM training'. Wageningen Agricultural Univ. Papers 93-3, 1993. (Doctoral dissertation.)
Food and Agriculture Organisation of the United Nations (FAO),. 'FAO's Plan of Action, Women in Agricultural Development'. Rome, 1990.
International Rice Research Institute, 'Women in rice farming'. Proceedings of a conference on Women in Rice Farming Systems. Hants (UK), Gower Publishing Company Ltd., 1985.
Kingsley, M.A. and S.S. Siwi, 'Update on women farmers' access to IPM activities: gender Study I Update Report'. Jakarta, Indonesian National IPM Programme, Ministry of Agriculture/Food and Agriculture Organisation of the United Nations, 1996. (Internal report.)
Pincus, J., 'Farmer Field School survey: impact of IPM training on farmers' pest control behavior'. Jakarta, IPM National Programme, 1991. (Internal report.)
Röling, N.G., Extension science: information systems in agricultural development. Cambridge, Cambridge University Press, 1988.
Sajogyo, P., Peranan wanita dalam perkembangan masyarakat desa. Jakarta, CV. Rajawali, 1983.
Shiva, V., Staying alive: women, ecology and development. London, Zed Books, 1989.

Siwi, S.S., M. Machmud and M. Mardiharini (eds.), 'Indonesian women in rice farming systems'. Proceedings of the first national workshop on Women in Rice Farming Systems in Indonesia. Bogor, Agency for Agricultural Research and Development, Central Research Institute for Food Crops and International Rice Research Institute, 1990.

Sumayao, B.R., 'Training the village non-traditional extension audiences on integrated pest management'. In: Filipino women in rice farming systems. Los Baños, U.P. at Los Baños, IRRI and the Philippine Institute for Development Studies, 1986, pp. 211-216.

Nguyen Nhat Tuyen[1]

8 Women in Vietnam's National IPM Programme

Vietnam is an agricultural country with a population of 74 million people, of whom 80% live in rural areas. Vietnamese women play a very important role in the national economy. More than 80% of those of working age (16–55) are engaged in economic activities outside the home. These workers make up 51.4% of the total labour force. Traditionally, Vietnamese women participate in many kinds of work, but their role in agricultural production is especially important: the majority work in the agricultural sector, which employs 72% of the total female labour force in the national economy as a whole (General Statistical Office, 1993). Of the 12 million farming households in the country, about 3 million are female headed. In accordance with local customs and traditions, the degree to which men and women share work differs among regions, but women always do a great deal of the work, especially in seeding, transplanting, weeding, watering, harvesting and post harvest activities.

Integrated pest management was introduced in Vietnam in 1992 through the National IPM Programme, a government activity which received technical and financial assistance from the FAO Inter-country IPM Programme.[2] IPM Farmer Field Schools (FFS), which had been developed and successfully piloted in Indonesia (see Chapter 7 of this book) provided an appropriate model for IPM training. These field schools last for one crop season and allow farmers to develop basic knowledge and skills on how to grow a healthy crop and prevent and control pests. Presently, IPM Farmer Field Schools have expanded nationwide.

In Vietnam, gender issues have been a concern of the National IPM Programme from the beginning. Efforts have been made to involve both men and women farmers in IPM Field Schools. However, women's participation had been less than men's, even though the shift away from cooperatives (outlined below) made women's involvement even more important. In the new situation women with less training became involved in pest management. Also, both women and men missed the opportunities for training that had been available to all farmers in the cooperatives. This paper discusses results of a study on Women and IPM in Vietnam implemented by the Center for Family and Women's Studies, Hanoi, for the Vietnam National IPM Programme. The purpose of the gender study was to look at women's participation in this programme and the constraints on their participation in Farmer Field Schools. The study was conducted in 1994 in three different geographical regions: the North, the Centre and the South. As a result of the data analysis, several recommendations were made to the leaders, staff, trainers and local representatives of the National IPM Programme. Further, the programme developed a module on gender issues for Training-of-Trainers courses.

Gender in agricultural activities

Division of agricultural labour

In Vietnam, women traditionally perform specific work. In rice production, women are perceived as doing 'light' work while men carry out 'heavy' tasks. This stereotype leads to the under-valuation of work done by women: in practice, despite the traditional gender division of labour, women have always done a great deal of heavy physical labour alongside their traditional roles. However, women's work has not been considered important due to the gender-biased value system. For example, studies conducted by the Agricultural Department of the National Economic University show that the payment for one work day of ploughing (done by men) has always been double the payment for a work day of transplanting, watering, weeding and so forth (done by women) (Hong, 1988).

Before the 1980s, during the cooperative period, plant protection was the responsibility of the cooperative, the plant protection staff and in some places extension workers. The members of the plant protection brigades were mostly young men and women farmers. They were responsible for spraying pesticides in the areas cultivated by the cooperatives.

Table 1 presents data derived from a survey of 104 farming households in one commune in the Mekong River Delta. In farm households, both men and women carry out plant protection work. A larger proportion of women than men are in charge of transplanting, tending crops, harvesting and raising pigs and livestock. Ploughing is the only activity in which women are seldom involved, as up to 55.7% of families hire wage labour for this purpose. Women also participate widely in potentially hazardous activities like spraying pesticides and applying fertilizer. Studies in other parts of the country have shown similar divisions of labour in families, although there are some small differences in the levels of women's and men's participation in specific types of work. Women in the North were observed to play major roles in agricultural production. This is a result of the many years of collectivization of farmers in the North, when men and women participated equally in agricultural work. However, women are everywhere primarily responsible for tending crops, harvesting and raising livestock. As mentioned above, women take part in virtually all stages of cultivation. The larger the size of a paddy plot, the higher the proportion of work done by women. They also do more work in diverse cropping systems than in monocropping systems. Girls participate in the production process from an early age (Thai, 1994). The results of a survey in Omon done by Can Tho Agricultural University (1993) demonstrate that women probably provide the principle source of labour in rice drying, weeding and transplanting. Women are also usually the ones hired for weeding and harvesting. In cultivation of subsidiary crops, in addition to weeding and drying seeds women undertake a high proportion of winnowing, watering and pesticide spraying work, especially in households where male members are absent.

Access to extension services

In Vietnam, the Extension Department and the Plant Protection Department are responsible for extension and plant protection services for farmers at the level of the commune. In the main rice cultivation regions – the Red River and Mekong River Deltas – extension services in districts are provided by staff of the extension department and plant protection department. The main activities of extension programmes are training, demonstration of technologies and pest management in communes. However, in remote areas there is a lack of extension staff. Ministry of Agriculture and Food Industry surveys of 35 cooperatives, production groups and cooperation teams have shown 100% male leadership. Nearly all extension workers operating at the field

Table 1 Division of agricultural labour in Mekong Delta households[a]

	Work done by					
	Wife	Husband	Both	Children	Other family members	Hired labour
Ploughing	0.3	19.0	6.3	10.0	2.5	55.7
Rice seed selection	26.2	36.1	0	28.2	11.5	0
Transplanting	37.0	5.5	3.5	23.3	4.1	24.7
Tending crops	32.4	16.2	20.6	20.6	5.9	4.4
Fertilizer application	25.4	36.6	0	25.4	12.7	0
Spraying pesticides	15.7	44.3	0	28.6	11.4	0
Harvesting	22.5	8.5	19.7	22.5	5.6	21.1
Gardening	10.0	30.0	40.0	10.0	10.0	0
Raising buffaloes/cows	11.5	26.0	25.0	25.5	12.3	0
Raising pigs	78.2	5.5	10.9	3.6	1.8	0
Treating livestock diseases	32.4	32.4	0	24.3	10.9	0

[a] N = 104 farm households
Source: Center for Family and Women's Studies, 1994

level are men, who were previously members of cooperative technical teams (Nguyen, 1994); only a handful of extension workers are women. The agricultural land policy reforms implemented in the late 1980s have given farm households the right to use the land allocated to them and to become independent of the cooperative. Farmers can decide whether to buy the services provided by the cooperative or not. In most cases, farmers tend to carry out plant protection work themselves, to reduce production costs.

According to the 1994 Ministry of Agriculture and Food Industry survey, in 20 provinces, farm households stated that plant protection work carried out by plant protection brigades of the cooperatives and production groups is done well. Whereas 42.6% of farmers said they were using their services, 86.3% of respondents perceived the price for these services as relatively high; about 20% of farm households are poor and lack experience in production and in obtaining capital. These households, many of which are headed by women, cannot afford access to these agricultural services.

The 1994 survey demonstrated a very great demand for plant protection information and other agricultural extension among farmers. Before the introduction of IPM in Vietnam, farmers were not aware of the dangers of overusing pesticides. A survey of 1,700 households in five provinces in the Red River Deltas in the North, covering the use of chemicals and fertilizer, showed that the average farmer used pesticides and chemical fertilizers, often storing them in the kitchen (Le, 1994). Few, but still some, farmers broadcast pesticides by hand. In families without men, even lactating women have to spray pesticides.

Need to involve women

In the period of transition from a centrally planned to a market economy, both women and men farmers face many difficulties. The collapse of the cooperative system means they are responsible for the land they have been allocated. Agricultural support services are no longer for their common use. Therefore, farmers need to be trained in crop protection methods, especially those that prevent a pest population from building up: how to grow a healthy crop, apply cultural practices, manage soil fertility and water, and select suitable varieties. Since the majority of farmers are women, they – and especially women in female-headed households – must have access to this training. Also, in Vietnamese culture, women are the ones who transfer farming knowledge to children at a very early age. Evidence has shown that women who attend IPM Farmer Field Schools usually explain what they have learned to their children and go through the life cycle of pests with them at home. Yet even though women are directly involved in many stages of the agricultural production process, their 'technical' knowledge of agriculture is very limited. As will be discussed below, they are often refused training because of their low educational level. In addition, there is a mentality that considers technology a male domain. Women therefore usually succeed principally as a result of hard work and experience.

Women and the National Programme

The national programme

Vietnam joined the FAO Inter-country IPM Programme in 1989. However, IPM activities began to develop and expand on a nationwide scale only in 1992, following the first national IPM meeting. The objective of IPM training is to enable farmers to develop the knowledge and skills needed for improved and informed decision making, based on a better understanding of the rice ecosystem. In IPM Training-of-Trainers, the hope is that trainers will gain skills that will help them to act as facilitators,[3] encouraging farmers to learn from their own experiences and research.

Vietnam's National IPM Programme is implemented by the Plant Protection Department (PPD) of the Ministry of Agriculture and Rural Development. Initially, national level trainers in the National IPM Programme came from the PPD; later on, farmers were also trained to serve as trainers of other farmers. Training-of-Trainers (TOT) and training for farmers are the core activities of the IPM programme. During TOT, participants learn the training skills and techniques needed to organize and facilitate Farmer Field Schools. After attending TOT, the trainers organize FFS in their provinces.

By the time of the autumn crop in 1995, there were 1,251 IPM trainer/facilitators in Vietnam, of whom 422 (33.7%) were women. The National IPM Programme had created new opportunities for women trainers, but it still faced a challenge: women also need to be more integrally involved in the IPM programme. This should include better representation of women in the leadership of the Plant Protection Sub-Department at all levels.

Women as trainees/participants

Statistics from the first IPM training cycles showed that the percentage of women participants in both TOT and FFS was small; it was not consistent with their level of participation in agriculture. Up to the autumn season crop of 1995, 36,905 farmers participated in FFS in the country as a whole; of these 8,466 (13%) were women, even though they make up 53% of total farm labour (National IPM Programme, 1995).

The participation of women varies across geographical locations, in accordance with local customs and gender relations. The biggest differences are between the North, with 36% participation, versus the Centre and the South, with 7% and 8% respectively; the average for the country is thus 13%. Some FFS groups in the South had only one female participant, who was the representative from the Women's Union in the village. During the field study in Tien Giang Province, many male interviewees said that women were not farmers, they usually do minor farming tasks. It was also observed that quite often it is only men who attend meetings and the training organized in or outside their village. In the Centre and in the South, stereotypes regarding the division of labour in farming and community work is a major constraint on women's participation in IPM activities.

Critical factors influencing women's participation in FFS

The gender study conducted by the Center for Family and Women's Studies for the National IPM Programme identified a number of factors that affect women's participation in Farmer Field Schools (CFWS, 1994a).

Time
One difficulty facing women who are potential trainees in courses like the FFS is how to arrange their time at home and work. Time management is the main factor that concerns rural women in general; therefore it must be considered when they are asked about the possibility of attending an IPM training. Time is scarcer and thus more 'costly' for the poor, and especially for widows and women with small children.

In addition to the work they must do in the fields and the house, they often have non-farming jobs such as trading or work for others to increase their income. If the time spent on the training course were to be significantly compensated, it could motivate more women in the lowest income group to attend.

Support from families
Most women farmers who responded favourably to questions about their participation in the IPM training course emphasized the support received from other members of their families. Men's participation in training courses is mainly the result of a personal decision; in contrast, women's participation is somewhat dependent on a collective decision by the whole family. A woman has to spend more time convincing other members of her family of the usefulness of her participation, encouraging them to understand and gaining their moral and practical support. For women, the most important support was shown in the specific attitudes and behaviour, either moral or practical, of other family members. The attitude and support of her husband are especially significant for her participation in the training course.

Involvement of local leaders
Village leadership, including the village administration and cooperative management, have important roles to play related to IPM training courses. Without their support and active involvement, most likely it will not be possible to successfully organize such training – or perhaps not even to hold it at all. Not only will their interest encourage families to have someone take part, but also local leaders are critically

important in the selection of participants. It has become clear (as discussed further below) that if more women are to participate, two elements will have to be agreed with these leaders during the preparation of an IPM course: the criteria for selecting participants (including the degree to which these will favour women), and the selection process to be used.

Specifically including mass organizations like the Women's Union at village level in the planning phase can also be a factor in making the most of women's participation. In addition, their involvement in identifying trainees helps to prepare for follow-up activities in which the training is consolidated and spread to others.

Procedures for participant selection
The selection procedures applied in the National IPM Programme differ from place to place, but during the gender study there were few instances in which this issue was raised in discussions between IPM trainer/facilitators and local leaders before the training began. In most cases the list of FFS participants was drawn up by the leaders of the locality. FFS participants are usually experienced farmers who meet the following criteria:
• completion of secondary school;
• experienced in farming;
• able to transfer knowledge and information to other farmers (to provide farmer-to-farmer training).

These criteria do not favour women's participation in IPM training. In many places, especially in the South, the role of women in agriculture is not visible; and in all parts of the country women are seen as poorly educated people who would not be able to speak in public, which is seen as a main criterion for selection. This has produced the situation in which the percentage of women participants is much lower than the percentage of men, especially in the Centre and in the South, where women are usually not fully recognized as farmers.

IPM trainer/facilitators
If a training event is to meet the requirements of both male and female farmers, trainer/facilitators should have a core role in its organization, because:
• trainers understand the objectives and significance of the IPM programme in general and the objectives and significance of the FFS for farmers, and female farmers in particular;
• trainers can create opportunities to meet local leaders on an equal, mutually respectful basis of understanding, and to discuss all issues related to training including the percentage of female trainees to be involved;
• trainers' attitudes, behaviours and training methods, as well as the way they co-organize a training course, can have a positive effect on the ways local leadership and both male and female farmers perceive issues related to gender.

However, at the time of the gender study, trainers were finding it difficult to take a more active role in trying to involve more women in FFS. In most cases they tended not to interfere; they did not see convincing village leadership of the necessity to include female trainees as their function. (Some trainers were also influenced by prevalent ideas on women's lack of capacity for participation in IPM training, and still did not recognize the importance of their participation.) Also, it appeared that trainers needed more information on the gender division of labour in the locality and on local mass organizations[4] such as the Women's Union, which represents women's interests. They also needed more negotiating skills. Without these elements, it was difficult for both male and female trainers to discuss the necessity of women's involvement in FFS with local leaders.

In addition, female trainers had other difficulties. For example:
• female trainers are 'less mobile'. If there is only one motorbike in the family, the husband, not the wife, uses it;
• their responsibilities in the family are greater than those of their husbands, so that they must be more skilful in managing their time.

Nevertheless, the presence of female trainers can create a favourable environment for attracting female farmers to an FFS. Female trainees see female trainers as examples, which can increase their self-confidence. Moreover, many female trainees expect it will be easier to communicate and talk openly with women trainers. The presence of female trainers can also help to change local leaders' perception of the capabilities of women.

Training organization and methods
In addition to the constraints above, when the gender study research team talked with trainers in various regions it became clear that they still lacked the practical skills needed to integrate gender awareness in the IPM-specific activities carried out within the FFS training programme. First, there were questions concerning the time period planned for the training event: is one crop period enough to allow trainers to meet the gender requirements, or is a longer period (such as one year) necessary? Second, the methods to be used in a training course with a higher number of female trainees are different and are aimed at encouraging gender awareness among both male and female participants and at making the most of women's participation.

Conclusions

The gender study results described above suggest the following conclusions.

• Women farmers' active role in agricultural production makes their participation in FFS necessary. At the time of the gender study, the involvement of women in the IPM programme was often due to the initiative of individual staff and trainer/facilitators, who worked with decision makers in the process of participant selection. FFS selection procedures need to be improved so that they reflect a better understanding of the real role of women in agriculture.

• Gender training courses are needed to increase gender awareness among the staff of the National IPM Programme, and a gender training manual needs to be developed to provide IPM trainer/facilitators with gender analysis and other related skills. This would help to give programme managers and FFS trainer/facilitators a better understanding of the effects of gender roles and the constraints on women's participation. As a result, IPM programmes would better reflect the needs of women. This sort of support could help trainer/facilitators and local leaders to understand the real roles and responsibilities of men and women in their communes and the way the present selection of training participants (with stereotype-based requirements related to educational level and communication skills) presents a major obstacle to involving women in FFS. A system of gender quotas could be set up, but this would only make sense if it were combined with appropriate methods for the creation of more gender awareness and sensitivity among trainer/facilitators and IPM staff. To translate these policies into practice, it will be necessary to integrate gender issues into the policies and activities of the National IPM Programme; a plan of action will be needed.

• In implementing the programme, there had not yet been effective coordination and collaboration with mass organizations, especially the Women's Union. The advantages of working with existing women's networks and activities to achieve better programme implementation have not yet been explored. Although a representative from the Women's Union attended a TOT, the Programme Coordination Committee had not sought the participation of the Women's Union. During the gender study some assistance from the Women's Staff Training School of the South was seen when they carried out an IPM training course for trainees of the school. However, this was incidental, and thus far the course has not been assessed to draw lessons or start a discussion on further cooperation with the school.

Recommendations

The gender study resulted in several recommendations to the Vietnam National IPM Programme, most of which are presently being implemented. These include the following.

National IPM Programme

• It is important to work out an action plan for integrating women into the IPM programme at national and local levels. This should include:
- targets to be achieved, including increases in the number of women trainers and in the PPD in general;
- plans for funding and implementing the action plan;
- plans for appointment of a task force and gender focal point staff to implement gender related activities;
- development of a gender training manual for IPM trainer/facilitators to increase skills in gender analysis and related areas and a manual/guidelines they can use in approaching villages, plus specific examples of activities for use in FFS;
- plans for an evaluation of the implementation of the action plan and a summing up of the lessons learned.

• In implementing IPM activities it is essential to establish cooperation with mass organizations at local level. Representatives of these organizations need to be involved in the process of selecting FFS participants and in organizing IPM clubs after training. The role of each organization in involving women in IPM activities should be made clear, and there should be a specific strategy to achieve training objectives.

Organizing the FFS

• To understand the needs of women and men farmers – so that appropriate methods can be chosen for approaching, selecting and training them – trainer/facilitators, the local authority and local representatives of mass organizations should carry out a gender analysis. This will provide a baseline showing the gender division of labour in the locality before an FFS is organized. This analysis can serve as a basis for trainer/facilitators, local authorities and mass organizations, giving a better picture of the work and lives of the local people who will be trained, and the aspects of their cultural background that present either obstacles to be overcome or opportunities to facilitate training. It can also help to define the appropriate percentages of men and women participants.

- The local population needs to be well informed about the IPM training in their community so they can understand what is happening and be aware of their possibilities for participating in it.

- Follow-up activities are very important for the sustainability and dissemination of IPM activities after formal training has been completed. There should be diverse forms of activities, including those suitable for women's participation.

Trainer/facilitators

- FFS trainer/facilitators need gender training as a part of TOT. This should serve to raise gender awareness and increase their skills, enabling them to implement gender analysis in localities where FFS is to be organized. Further, they need skills and methods that will help them to approach and work with local leaders, to involve women in the FFS, and to encourage women participants to take part in discussions and in FFS IPM activities.

- A manual for gender training is needed for TOT, including gender sensitive exercises on the roles of men and women farmers and the role women play in transferring farming knowledge to future generations.

Monitoring and evaluation

- Regular reports on FFS activities are important. Gender indicators for IPM should be established, to make it possible to measure the progress of the involvement of women in IPM activities, both as trainers and participants. FFS data should be gender disaggregated, and should note the difficulties or benefits of involving women in FFS. Reports should also give information on the coordination of FFS activities with other organizations in the locality, including extension training and plant protection related issues and the level of women's participation in these activities.

- A seminar on women and IPM should be organized to discuss and assess the results to date and decide if it is necessary to work out new strategies for integrating women: at the national level, as national IPM officers and leaders in the Plant Protection Department, as well as at the local level, as FFS trainer/facilitators, staff of subdivisions of the PPD or mass organizations and representatives of local authorities.

Notes

1 Many of the findings presented here are based on gender studies carried out by the staff of the Centre for Family and Women's Studies in Hanoi, Vietnam.
2 The Inter-country Programme for the Development and Application of Integrated Pest Control in Rice Growing in South and Southeast Asia of the UN Food and Agriculture Organization. Special funds were provided by the Government of Australia.
3 In Vietnamese, people who provide training are called 'teacher' by the participants. However, the ideal of training trainers to be facilitators is present. Here, a person who provides training is referred to as a trainer or facilitator. Similarly, women who attend training programmes are referred to either as participants or trainees.
4 Mass organizations in Vietnam include a very high percentage of the particular group addressed. Thus for example most women either belong to the Women's Union or to other organizations such as trade unions that are linked to it. The Women's Union is organized at national, provincial and local levels.

Bibliography

Can Tho Agricultural University, 'Data from a study in Omon', 1993. (Unpublished.)

Center for Family and Women Studies (CFWS), 'A preliminary study on the participation of women farmers in the IPM Programme in Vietnam', 1994a.

Center for Family and Women Studies (CFWS), 'Data from the research project "Participatory approach to a gender sensitive planning" ', 1994b. (Unpublished.)

General Statistical Office, *Statistical Year Book, Hanoi.* General Statistical Publishing House, 1993.

Hong, H. 'Economic relation between work norms in the new contract system and women's payment in agricultural cooperation in the Northern Red River Delta' Proceedings from a workshop on the Female Labor Force in the Red River Delta. Hanoi, Center for Women's Studies, 1988.

Le, T.N.T., 'Gender issues and agriculture under renovation conditions in Vietnam'. Paper presented at the National symposium on Integration of women in agriculture and rural development, organized by MAFI, FAO and NCFAW, Hanoi 5–7 December 1994.

Ministry of Agriculture and Food Industry, 'Data from a survey of the agricultural support system', 1994. (Unpublished.)

Ministry of Health, Vietnam, 'Unpublished statistics', 1992.

National IPM Programme, 'National IPM Planning - document from a policy meeting in Hanoi', 1994.

Nguyen, V.T., 'The need for effective assistance to improve the role of women in socio-economic development'. Paper presented at the National symposium on integration of women in agriculture and rural development, organized by MAFI, FAO and NCFAW, Hanoi 5–7 December 1994.

Thai, T.N.D., 'Role of women in agricultural production in Mekong Delta'. Paper presented at the National symposium on integration of women in agriculture and rural development, organized by MAFI, FAO and NCFAW, Hanoi 5–7 December 1994.

Frank H.J. van Schoubroeck, Cheki Wangmo and B.B. Acharya[1]

9 Gender aspects of IPM for citrus in eastern Bhutan

Bhutan, sandwiched between India and China, is one of the few remaining Himalayan kingdoms. In rural areas, villages of five to one hundred households are situated up to one day's walk apart in mountainous areas. In a few southern districts the culture of the predominantly Nepali speaking Hinduist groups is more reminiscent of the situation dominant in Nepal. Northern, central and eastern parts of the country are dominated by Buddhist Tibeto-Burmese speakers. Within these groups, men and women have comparable social, economic and political rights; some groups have matrilineal inheritance systems, and some accept both male and female polygamy. Killing any living creature is considered a serious sin in the local form of Buddhism. Female farmers outnumber male farmers: men are traditionally more involved in the clergy, the army and migratory labour. Increased standards of education have aggravated the 'brain drain' from agricultural activities; people with some education seek employment in the towns of western Bhutan or in the district headquarters. The country's rural economy is based on subsistence agriculture supplemented with cash crops (such as mandarin, cardamom, apple and potato), which are primarily exported to India and Bangladesh. Money is scarce in the villages of eastern Bhutan, but most daily needs are produced locally, so that few farmers handle it regularly. Yet money has its uses, and the local mandarin cultivation and trade is an important source of cash.

The agriculture sections of the twenty district administrations are the cornerstone of the agricultural extension services in Bhutan. Extension workers are based in their respective blocks, sometimes in remote block centres, from where they walk from village to village to carry out extension programmes. The district organizes yearly block level training, exhibitions and farmers' tours to which selected farmers are invited. Thus, the extension model is essentially a type of training-and-visit. The agricultural extension service officially targets households. Nevertheless, women were singled out in the Seventh Five-Year Plan (7FYP) (Anonymous, 1991): 'The involvement of women in development is one of the major themes of the 7FYP... to ensure that women are involved in the planning, implementation and management of the projects, including: agriculture...'. Since 1992, the extension policy of the Ministry of Agriculture has specifically included equal participation of both women and men in training programmes. Implementation depends mainly on the commitment of individual District Administrators and District Agriculture Officers, who generally sympathize with the policy. The district agriculture section invites equal numbers of men and women for block- or district-level training and for study tours if this is practical.

Mandarin is the major cash crop in Bhutan. The local (seed-multiplied, ungrafted) variety of *Citrus reticulata* has been cultivated for as long as people remember. Traditionally farmers exchanged mandarins for the salt and yarn they needed in the Assam and West-Bengal plains, a few days' walk from most citrus growing villages. In the 1960s the government started building roads, resulting in larger scale commercial citrus growing. Cash income from mandarin gained importance for large groups of otherwise subsistence farmers. Now, in citrus areas each household maintains ten to one hundred bearing trees. Thus, citrus pests have become more important, since they make yields low and irregular while losses affect profits rather than home consumption alone. In the late 1980s the government established a plant protection service, which began formal studies of citrus cultivation. Yields were up to six tonnes per ha (Fullerton, 1988), which is equivalent to 60 kg per tree. Some individual trees yielded 150–350 kg of high-quality fruit per year (author's observation), indicating the vast unused potential for improved yields. One key pest was the Chinese Citrus Fly (*Bactrocera minax*), which caused 30–80% premature fruit drop in infested areas. By 1994, the plant protection service had developed IPM based on protein baiting and hygienic measures, which required control efforts at village rather than household level (Schoubroeck, in prep.).

This chapter describes efforts to reduce losses by introducing IPM technology in citrus growing communities; the human aspects of IPM for Chinese Citrus Fly in villages will be the primary focus. An attempt is made to demonstrate the community organizational dynamics that made the programme succeed or fail, and women's key role in this. It is based on our experiences in implementing an IPM programme for citrus in eastern Pemagatshel and Samdrup Jongkhar districts. Rather than being based on an ideological choice in favour of women, gender-disaggregated information was used to achieve more effective programme implementation. Initially, in 1991–1993, the programme used a training-and-visit extension approach with some Farmer Field School (FFS) elements. We wondered: 'Are we reaching the people who actually take decisions on citrus management in a household? Are they changing their practices?' By 1994–1995 a pilot village approach had been adopted; this signalled a change in focus to main issues such as 'how can citrus growing communities implement IPM at communal level? How can agrotechnical and organizational know-how be introduced in 'outreach' villages?'

Development of a citrus IPM programme

From the early 1970s onwards, the extension service had addressed citrus cultivation by supplying seedlings and providing training on orchard management. Recommendations were apparently obtained from handbooks or from the practice of successful farmers, and were communicated in classroom situations, through lectures. Progress was measured in terms of the number of seedlings distributed and training sessions given. In 1991 the citrus IPM programme began, building on the existing training-and-visit practices of the extension service. For the citrus IPM programme we made adaptations, gradually incorporating elements of non-formal education approaches as applied in the Farmer Field School model developed for rice IPM in Indonesia (see Chapters 7 and 8). The training venue was changed from classrooms to orchards, and pest management terms were invented in the local language. Farmers were encouraged to practise recommended methods under supervision, and we repeated training during the pest development season. Farmers' progress was monitored by regular farmer interviews on knowledge and practices and on intra-household decision making; thus in monitoring, not only the number of people trained but also their improved knowledge and practices were considered. It was also at this point that we began to consider gender explicitly (see 'Why address gender...,' below, and the following sections). After two years of citrus IPM programme implementation, we could demonstrate that farmer's knowledge had increased. Their pest identification capabilities were better, and they knew more about life cycle characteristics and control strategies for key pests.

The earlier training-and-visit extension method had worked well for practices like improved pruning, planting and manuring practices, which are effective when carried out by individual farmers. However, even with the modifications, results were less satisfactory with respect to pest control. Farmers could see the utility of protein bait splashes, which should be carried out as the fly emerges, in April–May. However, it was also suggested that fruit drop (caused by the Chinese Citrus Fly) could be controlled by collecting and destroying the fruit that dropped in October–November, to eliminate maggots that would otherwise become a new generation of Citrus Fly in the next year. Such measures are only effective if strictly carried out by all citrus growers in a pocket. However, the effect will be visible only in the following year, and only a few farmers were willing to carry out control activities six months before a problem could be seen. In such a situation, it was not surprising that individual progressive farmers' activities had no apparent effect. The need for linkages between the technical properties of pests and the extension methods used became apparent to us, as well as the fact that a community of citrus growers could not be expected to adopt IPM for Citrus Fly after just a few lectures and demonstrations on the subject.

A pilot village approach

As the problems encountered made clear, there was a strong need to find ways to really embed practical IPM methods for key pests in village practices. We tried an unconventional extension approach. Instead of repeatedly training farmers on the technical aspects of Citrus Fly IPM, we initiated a control programme in one 'pilot village'. The primary goal was to develop an IPM strategy that was within farmers' reach. In the pilot village a researcher, an extension worker and a community of citrus growers worked together. The purpose, control of the Chinese Citrus Fly, was well delineated and served to structure the programme: every activity was directly related to this goal. For proper control of the Chinese Citrus Fly, farmers needed to know basic fly biology and understand concepts like natural control and principles of baiting. Researchers developed traps farmers could use to identify the proper time for bait splashing, and extension staff developed modules to make sure farmers understood the need for communal action (see photo). Programme staff and village leaders met regularly, and village meetings were held at key points in the pest life cycle. Through informal interviews with individual farmers, we monitored the willingness and ability of the community to jointly organize bait splashes and carry out hygienic measures. The initial work took place in 1993–1994; in the following years the programme was carried out by a stable group of farmers in the village. The objective was to continue organized baiting activity until the Chinese Citrus Fly population fell below damaging levels. Programme success was measured in terms of the level of communal activities and the losses due to Chinese Citrus Fly. In two consecutive years the programme resulted in the highest yields ever. After 1994, at the request of the District Administration, we organized outreach activities to neighbouring villages. In several of these villages, farmers managed to establish Citrus Fly baiting activities with similarly spectacular results.

Woman 'mandarin leaders' are often more successful than male counterparts in organizing communal baiting

Why address gender in an IPM programme?

Admittedly, when we began the programme, we were not interested in gender as such. Our aim was to increase mandarin yields. In daily practice the intentions outlined in the Seventh Five-Year Plan were rarely addressed explicitly. The term 'gender' entered the programme when a staff member of one funding agency took a particular paragraph in her job description seriously, insisting that gender be addressed explicitly in our citrus programme. Local administrators felt there was no sexual discrimination in Bhutan, and turned down proposals to specifically address women. To comply with the funding agency's wishes, we began to interview men and women separately about the gender-disaggregated division of labour and their programme participation. Looking back, using a gender perspective in interviews gave us significant insight into the local socioeconomic situation and helped us understand the relevance of the dynamics of village organization to our programme. Further, the success of women contact farmers and 'mandarin leaders' described below demonstrated that women are a very relevant target group for citrus extension in Bhutan.

Gender aspects of the T&V extension approach

Division of labour and participation in training

We collected gender-disaggregated data on the division of labour and control over benefits, and recorded participation in training and meetings (Table 1). People we had come to know personally in the first meetings were interviewed.

Table 1 Gender-disaggregated participation in citrus-related labour[a]

Activity	Statement on gender participation/recorded participation (%)			
	Women only	Men only	Both	N
Sowing	13	47	40	53
Planting	15	63	23	62
Weeding	25	29	46	56
Manuring	32	36	32	56
Pruning	13	82	4	45
Pest control	18	56	27	45
Harvesting	6	44	50	54
Transport	10	70	20	50
Sale	17	65	19	54
Keeping money	32	29	39	31
Training and meetings	67	33	-	1,500

[a] Training and meeting participation figures are based on the attendance recorded at each session; other data is based on interviews with 37 female and 32 male farmers, interviewed separately

Table 1 suggests there is no strict gender division of labour in citrus orchards: both sexes participate in orchard management, though men do more sowing, planting, pruning and pest management. Female farmers who said they had implemented plant protection measures were generally those explicitly trained by the programme. Handling and applying pesticides, if done at all, was usually done by the most experienced person (often male), as it was regarded as too risky for the average farmer. Male farmers were more involved in transport and trade: female farmers were less mobile due to reproductive tasks; women without young children were, like men, often involved in trade activities. Men and women had equal rights to the money earned, regardless of who received the money when selling produce.

Female participation in meetings and training was high: two-thirds of farmers attending training sessions were female. Households apparently sent people other than the actual implementors of the work to citrus training. Therefore we wondered whether trainees would discuss training contents at home after the meeting – does it matter who represents the household in these meetings? This had to be considered in the context of Bhutanese society. Informal observations suggested that greater exposure to outside influences is associated with greater literacy and public speaking ability. The person (usually a man) in whom these abilities were seen as more developed was apt to represent the household on public matters related to land- and water-rights, the national work force and taxes. For occasions seen as less important (such as IPM training), households often sent people whose absence would not interfere with daily work (grandfather/mother, women with young children who could not work on the land in any case). Farmers clearly saw their household as a unit, and felt represented in programme meetings if one household member attended. After training sessions, intra-household communication of training contents was poor. However, some people trained by the programme did begin carrying out orchard management as recommended, even if they had rarely worked in the orchard before being trained: within households, workers (both men and women) decided on work assignments among themselves; a given job was done by the person who recognized its relevance.

Though cash crop earnings were often collected by men, households spent money with the consent of all decision making family members. Most farmers stated that money was used for general household purposes (food, education, taxes), that there could be conflicts on expenditures, but that it is not automatically men or women who have the final say. Such attitudes may reinforce the typical Bhutanese view that development in general will benefit women as well as men.

Training National Women's Association members

During early stages of programme implementation, in 1992, there was an active branch of the national women's association (NWAB)[2] in Pemagatshel district. NWA members enjoyed an official status in their villages as 'woman village leader' or *Amchu tshokpa*. The Seventh Five-Year Plan suggested a type of 'gender-biased' extension: favouring women by ensuring that a set percentage of participants in training would be female. As a way of achieving this, the District Administration requested that the citrus IPM programme present orchard management training to members of the women's association (see photo). This lead to the establishment of female contact farmers in six villages. They had certain rights, including giving lectures during village meetings, but no administrative power; they could not independently organize communal activities in their villages. During later programme implementation, it was easy for programme staff to contact these women. In their villages they were regarded as citrus specialists and they actively took part in disseminating technical information within their villages. Due to the extended contact a trusting relationship developed between programme staff and the *amchu tshokpas*, who acted as key informants on the progress of the programme within the village.

Pilot village extension approach

Gender of programme staff

Up to late 1993, programme staff paid only brief visits to villages. Contacts with villages were mainly through the village leader or a familiar farmer, who called meetings and arranged food and shelter. The pilot village approach changed the relationship of programme staff with villages. In the pilot village, a network of farmers, extension and research staff was set up, we became more interested in community dynamics, and we had to reflect on our own role in the village – including the fact that, although an increasing number of female staff are employed, male staff dominate the extension service.

Citrus IPM training for women's association members in the district centre. As a result, women contact farmers were established in many villages

Knop and Knop (1994) found in Egypt that mixed staffing patterns facilitated work in villages. Female staff, however, did not necessarily have easier access to female farmers, in particular before developing personal relations within the village. In Bhutan, male and female, Bhutanese and expatriate staff are easily accepted as external experts. Particular behaviours such as refusing local welcoming drinks, a critical attitude towards local social habits and food, or unwillingness to give up one's status as 'outside official' will inhibit access to community dynamics. Staff who speak Sharchokpa-lo, the local language, can easily gain access to the community. For example, in most villages people enjoy a competitive game in which one party tries to win a debate with an opposing group. Such debates tend to develop between men and women during social functions – in our case between male extension staff and female farmers. The game helps build informal relationships between partners, which is a prerequisite for open discussions during later official meetings. Female extension staff rarely get involved in such sly debates as it could be harmful to their reputation. However, Sharchokpa speaking female staff can approach individual female farmers slightly more easily, and may have access to relevant information that does not come out during public joking sessions or official meetings. In our team, each member learned more about his or her role in interaction with the citrus growing community. For example, once our (male) team leader complimented a contact farmer in public for his excellent role in organizing baiting activities. He hoped the farmer would be stimulated by this public support. Later, a female member of our team talked privately with one of the village women, who said people did not like the fact that the contact farmer was given credit for work that was done by the entire community. Thus, the community taught the team leader in a quiet way that he needed to be more careful in complimenting individuals. The success or failure of programmes lay in understanding such subtle differences in behaviour. In general we found that for building a confidential relationship with male or female farmers, the sex of the extension staff was irrelevant in comparison to the value of speaking the local language and respecting local customs.

Chinese Citrus Fly baiting committees

During the earlier stages of the pilot village programme, we saw the study of intra-village dynamics as outside our mandate. We had expected to be able to simply explain Chinese Citrus Fly baiting to farmers, give materials and check the results of the experiments. This appeared to be oversimplified. Farmers carried out an incomplete bait splash programme in 1994, with disappointing control results. We found that this was due to low-profile opposition to the programme among local religious leaders (as it entailed killing insects), and we started to deliberately invite religious leaders to meetings where this aspect of IPM measures was discussed in comparison to chemical control. We proposed dropping the programme, which the community opposed; religious leaders assented that the programme was useful, though they did not personally want to be involved. It was decided to establish two Citrus Fly baiting committees, chaired by a *tshalu tshokpa* (approximately 'mandarin leader'), to organize Chinese Citrus Fly baiting for the 1995 season. The *tshalu tshokpa* was chosen by the community and had no official status, but the title *tshokpa* had an official connotation, giving the person a right to speak on mandarin activities in public meetings. The village was split into upper and lower parts; in each part a local committee was responsible for carrying out bait splashes. In the first year, the committee was supervised by extension staff and baiting was done meticulously, resulting in the highest yield ever.

The following year, we handed over responsibility for baiting to the two local committees. In the upper village baiting committee, the wife of the *tshalu tshokpa* organized baiting activities, but in the lower village, where the *tshalu tshokpa* was occupied with administrative work and family problems, control was insufficient. There were again heavy losses; people were now aware this was due to incomplete baiting. In 1997, the people of the upper village had to pay for new stocks of baiting material, while the lower village – though responsible for last year's losses – still had sufficient materials for the season's baiting activities. This, again, resulted in paralysis of baiting activities for the entire village.

The situation showed characteristics of a 'tragedy of the commons'. Individual farmers were powerless as long as the group as a whole did not get involved in setting a communal agenda. The few active women did not make use of their rights to push for such an agenda and were unable to successfully organize baiting activities. Smaller villages of six to eighteen households, however, surrounded the initial pilot village. Since they were aware of the mandarin programme in the original pilot village, from 1994 onwards these villages were willing to participate in outreach activities. The term *tshalu tshokpa* fit well in local organizational patterns and was copied in these villages. The villages were small enough for one person to organize baiting activities; in all but one, women were the 'village leaders' (see photo) in the other, a retired government official held this position. Baiting was properly carried out in 1995, 1996 and 1997 in all villages, and the Chinese Citrus Fly is now nearly eradicated. During the upscaling programme in 1995–97 this pattern was repeated in other places. In villages of more than about 20 households, individual active farmers could not carry out baiting activities alone; there was too much work for a single leader. In smaller villages, female *tshalu tshokpa's* in particular were remarkably successful in arranging for bait activities, which included collecting money to buy a stock of chemicals for the following year.

We are aware that we could be depicted as naive 'fans' of woman farmers if we were to simply state that women's success as *tshalu tshokpa's* was because they were more conscientious and worked harder in our programme. In fact their relative success can be understood by considering other groups of farmers. In remote villages, there were few active male farmers. They carried out various communal administrative tasks and were often temporarily away from the village. Lay monks made up an active and intellectually developed group of farmers, but could not be involved in pest control due to their religious status. Boys and girls with some education migrated out of the village and young women without children often left their village to follow a future mate. In remoter places, unmarried women with children (who could not migrate) and government officials (who had retired and returned) were the people available for involvement in technical programmes. In such villages, the two latter groups deserved the credit for the success of the citrus IPM programme. The programme not only resulted in improved knowledge within citrus growers' communities, but also gave a status of technical organizer to individual active women. In roadside villages, though, mandarin paid so well that some young men started trading rather than migrating to towns. In such villages, introduction of IPM went smoothly and we felt no need to study local community dynamics.

Two types of gender-sensitive extension

The training-and-visit extension approach used during the first two years of our programme provided a type of 'gender biased' extension: women received more training than their male counterparts. During training in villages, women's participation was high and there was no risk they would be systematically less informed than men. Women with small children could not easily leave home but still had access to extension programmes (see photo). The very fact that training was given in villages, in the local language, meant that all women could and did actively take part in training activities. At district level, women's association members learned about citrus IPM and practised speaking in public. (As noted earlier, men are more likely to become self-confident as they often live outside the village for longer periods.) Given such improved technical and social skills, women's structural public influence is likely to increase. This 'gender-biased' extension policy was a relatively simple adaptation of extension practices that are common in Bhutan. Therefore, it can be implemented quickly for large groups of farmers. Moreover, there is ample support for this approach within the agricultural extension service.

The extension approach used in the pilot village, on the other hand, provided 'community-sensitive' extension; in these villages, the programme dealt with

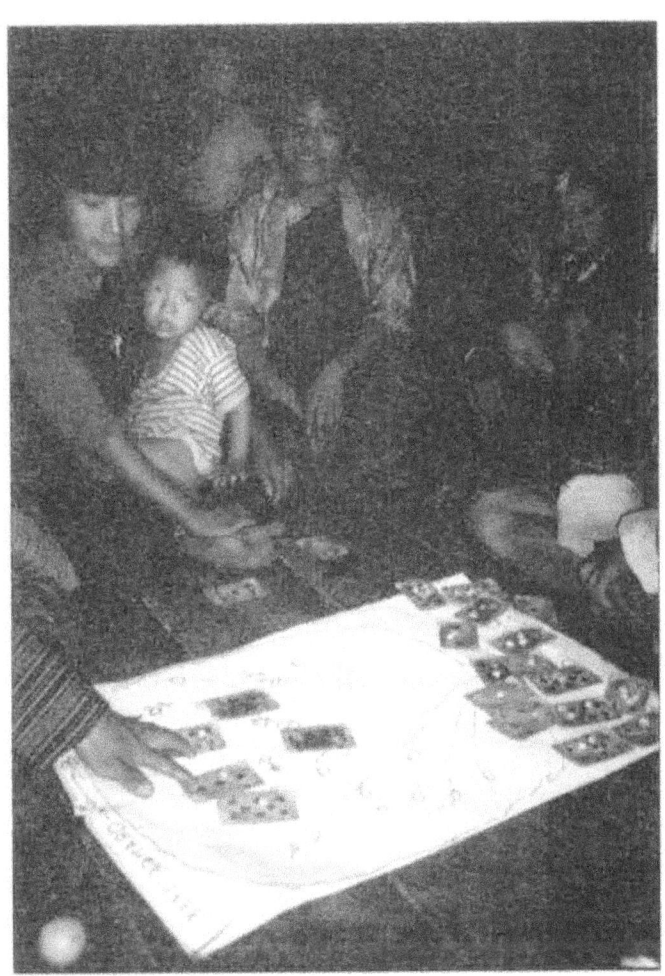

Extension activities in villages, carried out in the local language, are within women's reach

community aspects of IPM. As in the training-and-visit approach, women were reached in the villages where they lived, but in the pilot village approach we were also much better able to support the organizational activities of active farmers. Initially, women were clearly hesitant about active participation in baiting committees. The idea of inexperienced people, particularly women, putting themselves at the centre of public attention is not well regarded. During our regular and longer stays in villages we could identify people who were interested in active participation in the programme. If we knew someone was eager to join the activities, we would first discuss possible work personally, and later propose his or her candidacy for a function in a meeting. This made it possible to ensure that recommendations were indeed carried out within our experimental purpose. Some less mobile women (with young children) were a great help to the programme. After successful pest control, these women acquired the status of technically well-informed farmers with easy access to supplies of inputs and information from the extension service. They also received a great deal of public credit for their work. When the programme was over, each individual female *tshalu tshokpa* requested us to arrange for follow-up programmes '...to further develop the community'.

The community-sensitive approach is labour intensive and requires implementors to have social and language skills, but also it makes extension work a less formal, more enjoyable experience. Community-sensitive programmes serve many objectives of agriculture extension programmes (such as development and exchange of knowledge, and community organization). They increase growers' control over the crop and help less mobile farmers develop themselves intellectually and socially.

At present, the pilot village approach is being used by research programmes in Bhutan in various forms (for example, in the model schemes of the irrigation programme, which actually preceded our pilot village approach; and in key block and watershed agricultural research programmes). So far, approaches such as that used in the pilot area are seen as a means to more closely connect research to agricultural practice. However, the technologies that emerge from such research approaches call for an extension approach other than the dominant training-and-visit system. We therefore expect that these approaches too will gain ground in Bhutanese extension programmes. As a result, less mobile female farmers may come to profit from the social and intellectual challenges provided by such programmes.

Notes

1 We are grateful to Dasho (Dr.) Kinzang Dorji, Deputy Minister, Ministry of Agriculture, and Sherub Gyeltsen, Acting Director, REID, for their far-sighted leadership in general, and their kind permission to publish this material in particular. We also thank Dasho Penden Wangchuk for his heartwarming support for the programme in Pemagatshel district. The work received financial support from the Royal Government of Bhutan, the Commission of the European Union and the Netherlands Development Organisation (SNV). Mrs. Annet Noten initiated and actively supported the study of gender aspects in the programme. Mr. L.N. Sharma carried out fieldwork in the initial years of the programme. Farmers of Dungmin, Dena Woong, Martshala and Bainang Zor and Mikuri (Dungmin gewog), Jorphung, Kalishong and Thongsa (Chongshing gewog), Khar, and Am Shing (Gomdar gewog), carried out the programmes in their villages. Finally, we would like to thank Dr. H.R. Feijen, who played an essential role in programme planning and always supported us.
2 The national women's association of Bhutan (NWAB) is a non-governmental organization with branches in most districts.

Bibliography

Anonymous, 'Seventh five-year plan (1992-1997). Vol. 2. Project profiles'. Thimphu, Bhutan, Royal Government of Bhutan, Ministry of Planning, Planning commission, 1991, 210 pp.

Fullerton, R.A., 'Citrus production in Bhutan: a practical guide to improved husbandry and increased production'. EEC consultancy report. Thimphu, Bhutan, 1988, 34 pp. (Available from the National Plant Protection Centre (NPPC), Simtokha, Bhutan.)

Knop, E. and S. Knop, 'Addressing full-family dynamics in rural development'. In: Feldstein, H.S. and J. Jiggins (eds.), *Tools for the field: methodologies handbook for gender analysis in agriculture.* Connecticut, Kumarian Press, 1994, 270 pp.

Schoubroeck, F.H.J. van and M. Kool-de Rie, 'IPM for the Chinese Citrus Fly. I. Trapping and proteinaceous baiting'. Submitted to: *the International Journal of Pest Management.*

Janice Jiggins[1]

Epilogue

The collection of cases in this book is in equal measure inspiring and depressing. Many contributions are a happy record of the commitment of both women and men to developing and implementing approaches to small farmers' crop protection requirements – approaches that are not dependent on heavy use of toxic chemicals. They are depressing because they also record the specific ways women on the farm are affected by the use of toxic chemicals, and because, after over thirty years of active international and national lobbying, training and practical effort, it is clear that gender analysis has not become routine in the agricultural and scientific professions.

Yet, as Feldstein and Jiggins wrote in 1994, 'gender analysis adds a lot of insight for the production system as a whole and the understanding of opportunities for technological innovation' (p. 3). Gender analysis reveals the *diversity* of women's tasks and relationships within the family, on the farm, and in the wider agricultural environment and community, and the implications for crop protection strategies. The case studies from Russia, Ghana, Vietnam and Indonesia bring this out particularly well. It is worth pondering why, then, on the evidence of this book, today's generation of researchers is once more proposing an analytic focus on the family. The 'family' is where we, an older generation, began our challenge to the complacent, undifferentiated assumption made by farm economics, of a compliant domestic labour force under the direction of male household heads. The focus moved to 'women', as actors in their own right, making their own 'return to investment' calculations with respect to their labour power and their social, reproductive and economic obligations. And thence to 'gender relations' as a more powerful analytic term, providing insight into the relational quality of the economic, sociocultural and power dimensions framing the technical potential of agriculture. From the cases presented, it appears that the argument for renewed emphasis on the 'family' is not an analytic argument so much as a reaction to the environmentally and socially destructive forces of unrestrained market capitalism, of which the continued promotion of Class 1 toxic chemicals in agriculture is a particularly crass example. The devastating consequences are suggested in Chapter 1 by case studies from the Philippines, Malaysia and Pakistan.

The cases presented also document well the *fluidity* of gender relations. Women's and men's tasks and relationships, far from being unchanging cultural norms fixed in time, are evolving as macroeconomic forces impact village life. Unfortunately, as the studies from Honduras and Costa Rica suggest, the changes often seem to add to women's labour and responsibilities without necessarily bringing a commensurate increase in the quality of family life or livelihood security. In Russia, changes have been both abrupt and brutal, displacing women from the agricultural professions, restricting access to farm inputs including chemical pesticides, yet not offering viable, affordable crop protection alternatives.

The specific relevance of gender analysis to IPM lies in its power on the one hand to reveal why IPM programmes might fail to reach their maximum potential effect and, on the other, to suggest where opportunities for remedial adjustments to IPM programme design and implementation might lie.

Women interact with IPM in many ways. In most rural societies, women are connected to the household and the environment in ways men are not. Their specific roles in food production, processing, preparation and consumption, in family health care, and in the reproduction of the household through the daily round of chores as well as biological reproduction, tend to amplify the positive effects of including women as a part of planning for responsible management of the ecosystem, to say nothing of the impact of decreasing the use of toxic chemicals in crop protection.

Nevertheless, as a number of authors caution, in the absence of alternatives there are substantial risks in abandoning the immediate protection afforded by spraying with purchased chemicals. The difficulty in contrasting 'chemical' with other options, given that for instance the use of *neem* is itself a chemically-based option, lies in the imprecise specification of exactly what is undesirable about industrial chemicals. For example, the use of these chemicals sometimes trades immediate quantitative gains in yield and harvest security for a qualitative degeneration that compromises our longer-term future. If one analyses the pathways through which women's roles in production, household reproduction and biological reproduction shape the trade-offs and their costs, it becomes evident that IPM can be a powerful strategic intervention, with benefits far broader than the immediate crop-related gains. This also underscores the essential necessity of women's involvement in IPM implementation.

Further, such an analysis illustrates why the IPM message is not reducible to simple slogans such as 'don't spray', or to prescriptive recommendations. IPM seeks to turn negatives into positives, so that crop protection actively enhances the quality of ecosystem health, human health and household reproduction. Without the sustainable community life contingent on household reproduction (no matter how one defines 'community'), there can be no sustainable resource management. However, the management of qualitative states cannot be mechanistic or technocratic, or, differently stated, simply an intervention that breaks a negative relationship. It necessarily depends on enhanced powers of observation, measurement and interpretation of states that are both fuzzy and dynamic. Management of qualitative states thus importantly also involves new ways of communicating. The cognitive sciences provide strong grounds for promoting the specific combination and sequencing found in IPM – *individual* learning followed by *collective* review – as most likely to generate effective problem solving (Clark, 1997, Chapter 9). Moreover, there are strong grounds for seeking to create a new kind of external structuring of decision making, using mechanisms such as Farmer Field Schools. We can read the FFS as organizations that prompt and coordinate sequences of learning and decision making that match the dynamic of complex environments. Particular decisions can then be seen as partial or incomplete solutions that in turn inject further learning and feedback into subsequent cycles of problem solving.

In 1995, a review of integrated pest management in the tropics (Mengech, Saxena and Gopalan, 1995) concluded that two major bottlenecks would have to be tackled more forcefully if IPM as a 'sophisticated biologically intensive management system' were to secure sustainable yield at lower environmental and social costs on a larger scale. The two bottlenecks identified were first, the difficulties in developing IPM programmes in which all necessary components form a coherent system; and second, the difficulties IPM proponents may have in convincing others of the advantages. The essays in this book offer some comfort that the efforts of women scientists, women farmers and IPM advocates might together contribute to the resolution of these difficulties.

Yet since 1995, the risk of chemically-induced disaster, especially in regions such as Africa where uncontrolled use is rising particularly rapidly, has greatly increased as market forces continue to favour the use of high levels of chemical crop protection. On the other hand, the claims of bioengineers and chemical companies that in some crops the latest genetically engineered products offer complete protection at lower environmental cost would seem to warrant further investigation from an ecological perspective, since the wider systemic effects of preventing pest predation over large areas are largely unknown. For example, there has been concern about possible decreases in natural enemy populations in areas planted with crops engineered to resist pests. There is clearly much more work to be done, and I am sure many readers will look to the editors and authors of this volume to take on the challenge and report the results.

Note

[1] Professor of Human Ecology, Swedish University of Agricultural Sciences, Uppsala, Sweden.

Bibliography

Clark, A., *Being there: putting brain, body, and the world together again.* Cambridge, MA., The MIT Press, 1997.

Feldstein, H. and J. Jiggins (eds.), *Tools for the field: gender analysis in farming systems research and extension.* West Hartford, Kumarian Press, 1994.

Mengech, A.N., K.N. Saxena, H.N B.Gopalan (eds.), *Integrated pest management in the tropics: current status and future prospects.* Chichester, John Wiley and Sons, 1995. (Published on behalf of UNEP.)

About the authors

B.B. Acharya is an agriculture extension supervisor who worked in Pemagatshel district for six years. He carried out essential work for citrus IPM programme when he was stationed at Dungmin village in Pemagatshel.

Fadhila H. Ali is currently based at the Natural Resources Institute, doing research on the epidemiology of Rice Yellow Mottle Virus in the rainfed lowland systems of Tanzania. Ali is registered for PhD research at the University of Greenwich, UK. She is experienced in participatory approaches and has carried out consultancy work related to diagnostic surveys and evaluation of rice-based projects.

Since receiving a doctorate in ecology from the University of California at Davis, specializing in agricultural ecosystems, *Lisa Bradshaw* has spent several years in Central America as a member of interdisciplinary teams doing applied research in agroecology and conservation biology. Currently she is one of the resident faculty at the School for Field Studies Center for Sustainable Development Studies in Costa Rica. Her teaching and research program integrates ecological, economic and social aspects of local productive and conservation land use systems.

Elske J. van de Fliert is an extension scientist and ecologist. She obtained her PhD in Extension Science and Plant Protection at Wageningen Agricultural University, the Netherlands, in 1993. She has had extensive experience as a consultant for international, governmental and non-governmental organizations in areas related to sustainable agriculture, IPM and extension. She is currently the IPM Specialist at CIP for the East, Southeast Asia and Pacific Region.

Janice Jiggins completed a PhD in history at the University of Sri Lanka in 1974. Her extensive international teaching and research experience, including consultancies in many parts of the world, has primarily involved programme development in agricultural research and extension management, organization and technology development for small farmers, services for female farmers, reproductive health and population policy. In 1996 she was appointed professor in Human Ecology at the Swedish University of Agricultural Sciences, in Uppsala. Current interests include relationships among population dynamics, food supply and natural resources; systems thinking and soft methodologies; and the application of participatory approaches to ecological land use.

After earning an MSc in agronomy, specializing in Tropical Entomology, *Alida Laurense* spent 20 years in Sub-Saharan Africa as a lecturer in general entomology, applied entomology and ecology in southern Sudan and Niger; an associate expert in a Gambian IPM project, and an IPM training and extension expert in Zanzibar, Tanzania. Here the Plant Protection Division focused on developing appropriate IPM strategies for subsistence farmers, and more recently the introduction of a Farmer Field School approach. At present she is Team Leader of a Horticultural Project in

Fayoum, Egypt, especially engaged in training female extension workers to work with female-led small farms using the TOT/FFS approach.

Catrin J. Meir has submitted her PhD thesis 'Training for change: evaluation of participatory training in natural pest control for smallholder farmers in Central America', conducted with the Imperial College Centre for Environmental Technology, to the University of London. Catrin has an MSc in Environmental Technology (Ecological Management) and has undertaken consultancy work in extension and facilitation, as well as research, in Honduras, Nicaragua, Costa Rica and Ecuador.

Nguyen Nhat Tuyen is a sociologist who obtained her MA in Development Studies (Women and Development) at the Institute of Social Studies in The Hague, the Netherlands. She works as a staff member/researcher in the Methodology, Gender and Development Department of the Centre for Family and Women's Studies in Hanoi, Vietnam in the fields of rural development, technology and women.

After obtaining a doctorate in chemistry in 1972 (Lomonov Moscow Institute of Chemical Technology) *Natalia Leonidovna Poznanskaya* has primarily been active in the development of new crop protection chemicals. At present, she is chief of the chemical analysis laboratory at the Scientific Research Institute for Plant Protection Chemicals in Moscow.

Jet Proost has a background in rural sociology and extension science; she is an assistant professor in the department of Communication and Innovation Studies at Wageningen Agricultural University. She specializes in environmental issues in agriculture as well as the management of extension services. Her PhD thesis will be submitted by the end of 1999, with a central focus on the human dimension of change processes, moving towards more sustainable agricultural production systems. Her special interest is in farmer driven change and ways to support it. As an independent consultant she advises organizations on the participatory development and implementation of agricultural projects.

Sarojeni V. Rengam is Executive Director of Pesticide Action Network Asia and the Pacific, based in Penang, Malaysia. A zoologist by training, she has had many years of experience working on issues of pesticides and pest management. She is also very much involved in Women in Agriculture, one of the programmes undertaken by PAN Asia Pacific, and is the co-author of several publications in fields related to these areas.

Frank van Schoubroeck worked in Bhutan from 1990 to 1998, where he was involved in designing and implementing a Citrus IPM Programme. He developed IPM for a few key pests in a 'pilot village' setting, where he also developed methods to introduce IPM in citrus growing communities. Later he carried out an IPM extension programme, to scale up pest control activities. He is presently completing a Ph.D. covering his work in Bhutan at Wageningen Agricultural University, The Netherlands.

Sarah Jane Tisch completed her PhD in 1986 at the State University of New York at Binghamton with a major in international political economy. Her major field of work is international agricultural development, with a focus on women's leadership. At present she is Director of the Leadership and Human Development Program at Winrock International Institute for Agricultural Development in Arlington, Virginia, in the USA.

Brenda Joyce Vander Mey completed her MA and PhD studies at Mississippi State University, Mississippi (USA). Her major fields of work include farm family systems, whole farm system analysis, gender analysis, factors affecting the adoption of IPM and sustainable agriculture, environmental sociology, family sociology, public opinion on animal agriculture and gardening with at-risk youth. At present, she is an Associate Professor of Sociology at Clemson University in South Carolina, USA. She also is the Coordinator for the South Carolina Landscapes for Learning Collaborative.

Cheki Wangmo is a diploma holder who previously worked with the Citrus IPM Programme in Bhutan. She is now employed by the National Biodiversity Programme of Bhutan.

Jan C. Zadoks' PhD. thesis (University of Amsterdam, 1961) was on 'Yellow rust on wheat, studies in epidemiology and physiologic specialization'. He joined Wageningen Agricultural University, specialized in epidemiology, and became professor of ecological plant pathology in 1969. His research was primarily on cereal diseases; a 1974 scale for growth stages of cereals became the UPOV and FAO standard.

The (co)author of more than 400 papers and supervisor of more than 40 PhD. theses, he also carried out overseas consultancy missions for FAO and for the Netherlands and French governments (crop loss, resistance, IPM, teaching) and participated in reviews of DFPV, ICRISAT, IRHO and IRRI. Further, he was a member of the FAO/UNEP Panel of Experts for Integrated Pest Control, and organized the 13th International Plant Protection Congress in 1995.

www.ingramcontent.com/pod-product-compliance
Ingram Content Group UK Ltd.
Pitfield, Milton Keynes, MK11 3LW, UK
UKHW050523150426
5217IPUK00026B/1762